TESS CASTLEMAN

SACRED DREAM CIRCLES:

A GUIDE TO FACILITATING JUNGIAN DREAM GROUPS

For Curtis Castleman, 1917 – 2009

Tess Castleman

Sacred Dream Circles

A Guide to Facilitating Jungian Dream Groups

DAIMON
VERLAG

ISBN 978-3-85630-731-8

Cover photograph by Nicholas DeSciose

Contents

Part One: Gathering

Part Two: Foundations

Part Three: Depth

Part Four: Perspective

Part Five: Expertise

Part Six: The Sacred Circle

Acknowledgments

IN THE BEGINNING, SINCE JANUARY 1987, THE PARTICIPANTS IN MY dream circles have been generous, forgiving and faithful in walking with me on the path of discovering how dreaming together could grow and evolve.

In the middle, since 2004, my professional partner and friend, Dr. Jenny Gordon has been a confidant, a supporter, a critic and an invaluable aid in developing the dream retreats we have held together.

In the end, my colleague and friend, Dr. Nicholas French has been unbelievably clever, patient and magnanimous in edit suggestions that have made this book clearer and better to read.

Without the people mentioned here, this book certainly would not have come to be. Saying, "I extend my heartfelt thanks" nor any other phrase I know begins to express the appreciation and gratitude I have. I am fortunate beyond understanding to have such people in my life and work

Tess Castleman, 2009

Introduction

I HAVE BEEN LEADING DREAM GROUPS SINCE JANUARY 1987, AND they still fascinate me with their mystery, their synchronicities, and their power to change people through love's medicine. I have witnessed romantic love bloom, friendship flower, and the love between a teacher and pupil form a solid foundation for group dream work. Some of the magic that has occurred has actually been hard to believe. I am simply a witness, one of many, and from stories about other dream groups, I know that the same happens everywhere.[1]

Dream circles can take place in jails, nursing homes, or at junior high schools; they can be done in a dormitory, an office or in a family, and these are only a few of the possibilities. Many others have written about dream groups. What I offer is a Jungian analyst's approach: working with dreams from analytical, anthropological and cultural perspectives. I have included guidelines, most of which I learned the hard way, by making mistakes. Over the years, I have seen more than one dream circle member run out of the room screaming and crying, and several have disappeared without giving any indication of the reason for leaving. I have known members to scapegoat another member, or myself. These have all been learning experiences, valuable in the context of group process, though

1 Confirmed by personal conversations in Zürich, Brazil, Denmark, Dayton (Ohio), Portland (Oregon), Eugene (Oregon) and other locales, as well in emails, letters and phone conversations.

destructive in a dream circle. There are good reasons why dream circles require different rules than a group therapy process, and they cannot be over-emphasized. Lacking clear rules, dream circles can quickly become destructive and totally counter-productive.

When working with dreams, a circle member is laid bare, whether one realizes it or not. Dreams come from a deep and vulnerable place in the psyche. When exploring the imagery within a dream, a dreamer begins to probe elements of her unconscious that are tender and struggle to come to consciousness. The new material, as well as the one who dreams it, must be cared for like a green shoot in the first days of spring. Those of you who already work with dreams know this to be true; if you are skeptical, I can only ask that you trust my ideas. It is unethical to bring someone into a dream group, only to subject her to criticism, judgment and advice. Imagine treating a new artist with a first canvas this way. The process can fall apart quickly, and all of the courage and resolve it took to join a dream circle and to share a dream might be chased away, perhaps never to return.

Some Jungians have cautioned against group work. The reason is important: concern about "psychic infection," in which one person's unconscious affects another's to such a degree that multiple psyches seem to overlap and bleed together, and it is hard to determine one's personal boundaries.[1] Because Jungians are trained in the importance of the process of individuation (the slow, painful and ultimately revitalizing process of discovering one's unique, authentic self), group dream "layering" is considered neither safe nor desirable. When psychic infection occurs, it can be terribly destructive. War is one haunting reality, but on a smaller scale, one ghastly example occurred some years ago, when a group in California all committed suicide together, believing they would be transported into outer space to board the "mother ship."

1 Marie-Louise von Franz, one of Jung's most influential colleagues, was reported in the 1980's to have been particularly unhappy with her Jungian colleagues' interest in group work.

In one case in my private practice, an analysand "caught" a psychological disturbance from another patient at the hospital where they were both in-patients. One was a "cutter" (one who practices self-injury), and the other, who had not seen or heard about "cutting" before started doing it, too, when she learned about that behavior. Clearly, some psychic processes are contagious. In dream circle, one can defend against such disturbing outcomes by practicing the guidelines outlined in this book. While there can be no guarantees, because there are too many variable factors, most misfortunes can be avoided by developing a structure that provides a strong enough container that dream circles can focus instead on increasing their understanding, and developing connections between their members. This is the fascination of dream circles.

The magic can take a number of forms, and I am sure there are many I have not yet seen. Especially astounding are the synchronicities that can happen. They emerge with regularity in every possible venue: within the dream material, inside the content being discussed, outside or inside group, in parallels of dress, and in other surprises. Synchronicity is a subject that will be revisited several times throughout this book.

The nascent core of this work is the inspiration I received from the Native American people of the plains, the Lakota. This nation approaches unconscious material from a spiritual, relational and tribal viewpoint.[1] It is my hypothesis that this element is crucially lacking in therapeutic dream work, spiritual direction, church and temple experience, group therapy, family systems work and other group situations, including traditional analysis, where analyst and analysand create a contained, closed temenos for healing and insight.

I call this missing element the "tribal unconscious." In Jungian terms, this aspect of the unconscious resides between the personal

1 For more on the Lakota and their experience of dreams, see Neihardt, *Black Elk Speaks*.

unconscious and the collective unconscious. I see it as a significant, interactive field that is often ignored by traditional psychology. Jung touched on it, but did not fully articulate the point in his *Dream Seminar Notes*[1], when he differentiated between the subjective and objective dream. The subjective dream is just about the dreamer, and characters in the dream are all parts of himself. The objective dream contains material that is "accurate" in the waking world; these dreams present us with objective data that is realistic and informative. Some of these dreams are remarkable, providing predictive, insightful information that solves dilemmas or aids the dreamer in other ways. Others are synchronistic, providing the dreamer with startling coincidences that can alter his consciousness. Still other objective dreams are corrective: if I have too low an opinion of someone, I might dream in a compensatory way that corrects my attitude about that individual.

Part of the modern soul-less problem is the loss of tribal life and customs. Tribal consciousness is almost impossible for postmodern people to conceptualize or relate to, sort of like trying to imagine what it would be like to be an identical twin. The Boy Scouts, church, your neighborhood and the local Jung Society are not even close to living with others in such a community of perhaps one hundred teepees and souls who share your religion, dress, diet, customs, rites of passage and personal history. The tribe broadened this reverberating interconnectedness further when the Sun Dance brought together many tribes, distant cousins and new alliances in a phenomenal, deeply woven tapestry of history and shared tradition.

We have lost this sense of profound belonging. Political parties, the Bach society, the sailing club, none even begins to deal with the modern loss of soul and sense of existential alienation that have encouraged suicide, violence, drug use and a general weakening of depth and meaning in our society.

---

1 Jung, *Seminar on Dream Analysis: Notes of The Seminar Given 1928-1930*

Bringing the tribal field into consciousness may be a small step in the direction of healing individuals, relationships, groups and cultures, but it is where the dream world first takes us.

What is this Handbook About?

IT IS ABOUT YOU AND A FEW OTHER PEOPLE COMING TOGETHER to develop a dream group.

Why have you written this guidebook?

In part, it is because after *Threads, Knots, Tapestries*[1] was published, I was asked to teach people how to start their own dream groups. The handbook is also an outgrowth of retreats I have lead to facilitate people dreaming together in a group setting.

Why would people want to start a dream group?

Dream Groups have been an interesting experiment in my private practice as a Jungian analyst. In 1986, inspired by reading Lakota anthropological texts, I decided to bring people together to discuss their dreams. It was mind-expanding for me to discover that the First People of the American Plains felt dreams were not silly, not to be ignored and not only for individual dreamers, but that some were meant for the entire community to ponder and acknowledge with ceremonial significance. They knew that important dreams with certain characteristics needed to be told to the whole tribe, or misfortune could befall them. They also knew that dreams have impact on others who hear them, as well as the dreamer. Since my training as a Jungian analyst has given me valuable experience in

1 Castleman, *Threads, Knots, Tapestries: How a Tribal Connection is Revealed through Dreams and Synchronicities.*

working with dreams, putting individuals together to dream in a group setting seemed like a natural thing to do.

What happened?

Most of what happened is told in *Threads, Knots, Tapestries.* To summarize: I found that the members of dream groups became personally close, connected and loyal to one another, that dream material did affect most who heard it, and that dream group members manifested a "tribal unconscious" in which their dreams interlaced, overlapped and impacted one another.

Is this something people can try without a Jungian analyst?

Yes. However, I strongly urge that, if at all possible, each group contact a Jungian analyst or a Jungian-orientated therapist for some consultation, or, ideally, to lead and facilitate the group. To be a Jungian analyst, one must be certified by the International Association for Analytical Psychology (I.A.A.P.). You can find listings on the Internet, or you may write or email me for a referral.

Some analysts may not be comfortable doing group work, and that is certainly their prerogative. However, most, when introduced to my book and handbook, are quite willing to try a dream group, even if they are not already running one.

You may find that your group wants only an occasional visit, or an hour here or there, so your group may use an analyst as an occasional consultant rather than a facilitator at each meeting.

What do people who have been in dream groups say?

"Actively listening for symbols and metaphors in others' dreams has helped me better discern my own dream symbols."

"I found so many synchronicities when other people shared their dreams. My insights were far greater than I would have accomplished solo in the same period of time."

"Dream group is different than individual analysis, which I have engaged in over the years. In group the dream is let loose in the room and it forms a web of connection between the group members … "

Do we have to read the whole book from beginning to end or can we jump around and pick and choose?

Sacred Dream Circles is designed to be read from the beginning, each chapter roughly covering one dream circle session. Some chapters, however, may take several sessions for your circle to complete, since each group will vary widely. Going slowly, taking your time is my recommendation. Additionally, each chapter has at least one exercise to help anchor the concepts being addressed. Some groups might prefer to opt out of some exercises, but each one has been tested and found to bear productive results in analysis, dream circles and dream retreats.

Is it really possible to have this kind of success in a leaderless dream group?

Yes, it is. This is why Sacred Dream Circles was written: as an aide for analysts, therapists and group members with no training. Following the rules provided, all of which are discussed in this handbook, will make your experience worthwhile,

Good luck, and enjoy!

Part One

Gathering

photo: Len Blu

The Beginning

Materials needed: spool of thread, twine, or yarn, long nail, thin dowel, ice pick or thin instrument to run through the spool of thread so that is can spin easily, poster board or white fabric (like an old table cloth or sheet) pins, white glue, spray paints.

A: Introductions
B: Selecting a Leader
C: Structure
D: Rules
E: Opening and Closing Rituals

A. Introductions

Because dream groups involve intense self-discovery, and because they tend to create and intensify relationships, dream circles can be a little bit scary right at the beginning. Opening up to others as a way to grow is a new process for most of us, but it is essential to be frank and honest. As each individual opens up, others will feel more comfortable sharing their personal information as well. Dream group is a close, messy undertaking, so it is best to jump right in.

Please gather in a circle. When you introduce yourself, you should include your name, information about your work or special interests, and your family. You might also want to talk about your personal history, your family of origin, your present stage of life, your current concerns and your motivation for joining a dream group. Include something special that the group does not know or that you do not usually share in ordinary social settings.

As each person speaks, hone your listening skills. No interruptions, no questions, and no judging. Quiet and intent listening is all that is called for. If you are the leader, you need only to thank each person after his or her introduction.

You will discover, as common themes emerge, that a unique group has already begun to form. You may also find that several members are friends and that your dream group contains one or more subgroups[1]. A subgroup is a number of people who have been part of another group before this meeting, such as people from a yoga class or an office who are in the dream group together. Subgroups must be careful not to exclude new people from their history and intimacy. Subgroups might agree, for example, that they will not talk among themselves about the dream group, its members or the events in the group.

You can help your dream group unite by noting shared similarities and common concerns and by welcoming differences which add texture to the group and make it more interesting. The *glue* of your group will be the commitment each person makes to be supportive and to respect the integrity of the other members.

B: Selecting a Leader

Your group will need to elect a leader. A dream group leader is not a professional facilitator who will interpret dreams and lead the group process. A dream group leader is an administrator, elected by the group, who will call the members if there is a time change, act as a clearinghouse for new members' phone calls and deal with the housekeeping duties of the group. Your leader will not be a

1 Yalom and Leszcz, *The Theory and Practice of Group Psychotherapy*, p. 391

unilateral decision maker and will act only for the good will and the functionality of the group.

Your leader will take notes during the first meeting recording all of the decisions the group makes. He or she will pass around a name, phone and address list for all members to sign and ask for a volunteer to copy the list and hand it out at the next meeting, with a reminder that it is important for members to call if they are not able to come to dream circle.

C. Structure

At the first meeting, you need to decide when, where and how long to meet. Many successful groups have decided to meet every week for an hour and a half or every other week for three hours. Your group may decide to meet one day a month or twice a year over a weekend. The options are many and varied, and each group must decide how much time and effort to dedicate to dream work. The stronger your commitment, the greater your reward will be.

Your meeting place should be safe, comfortable and private. Groups that meet in homes may want to meet in one for a fixed period of time and then rotate to another home.

Your group should also discuss how many members to include. There is really no minimum, but there certainly can be a maximum. Usually a group over eight members becomes a bit chaotic. Limitation on membership may evolve over time as the group becomes more bonded.

Some of your most important decisions will involve how to organize dream group time. Will you take turns sharing dreams, or let members volunteer? While it is not necessary, I recommend that members agree to record their dreams thoroughly throughout the week and bring a written copy to share with the group. Not everyone will share a dream at every meeting, so it is advisable to allow time for each member to "check in," whether or not s/he is sharing a dream.

Finally, taking time at the beginning to discuss common issues that all groups encounter will make future meetings more successful. For example, what will your group do if someone "hogs" time or is too shy to participate?

D) Rules

Many of your group's rules will emerge from your individual decisions, but every dream group needs to honor the following essential rules:

1) Confidentiality

All matters that are discussed in the group must be strictly confidential. Because dream work requires sharing personal information, the dream circle must be a private container that is safe and secure. Everyone desires and deserves personal privacy, so there must be absolutely no talking about dream circle material outside the group, even without naming a person's identity. Any person known to have broken this rule should be dismissed from the group. In addition, each member should sign a confidentiality agreement[1] at your first meeting.

2) Commitment

Each dream group member will benefit from as strong a commitment to the group as possible. Three months is the minimum, and one year would be better. A dream group must form a consistent, reliable venue in which to share personal dream material. Each member needs to know that the others will be there next time, especially after having shared very private material. Of course,

1 See Appendix B

absences are not necessarily a sign of a lack of dedication; circles must be flexible as well as committed. If someone is not sure that dream group is really what he or she wants, then s/he needs to leave. Shopping around is not helpful for the group process and is even damaging to the essential bonding process that begins with the very first meeting.

3) Supportive behavior

When we share a dream and discuss the personal issues associated with a dream's content, we are vulnerable. For dream work to be successful, it is essential that each one of us feel we can share personal information without anyone giving advice or jumping to conclusions about the dream's meaning. Consequently, judgmental attitudes are counterproductive to any work with dreams. Empathetic listening *without intervention* is the goal of a dream circle. No criticism, no advice, and no interpretation. The interpretive phase of dream work will be discussed in later chapters.

4) Protocol for leaving the group

Most of us underestimate our importance to the group. Because dream work is intensely personal, strong bonds form in a dream circle. Simply disappearing from the group will leave other members feeling abandoned. Nevertheless, each person benefits most from following his or her own process, so it is better not to apply emotional pressure to a person who wants to leave. If you decide to leave the group, please inform the other members as soon as possible. You may leave simply because of a new job or change of residence, but if you are unhappy with the group, your evaluation could help to improve the group process. Eventually, every group should develop good-bye rituals as well as ways to deal with dissatisfaction in the group. This subject is dealt with in more detail in a later chapter, and will be useful after your group has had a chance to come together.

E: Opening and Closing Rituals

Your group may wish to develop opening and closing rituals, such as holding hands and forming a circle, lighting a candle, joining in a meditation, or a blessing[1]. You might decide to take turns opening and closing your meetings, or your group may be more comfortable without ritual and choose to be informal.

Congratulations, you have entered a journey of discovery with playmates, soul-mates, dream-mates. The following exercise is fun, creative and will begin to enhance your adventure together.

EXERCISE: THE THREAD TAPESTRY CREATION

You will need a spool of thread or ball of string with an opening in the middle, a large-headed nail, swizzle stick, ice pick, eyebrow pencil or other thin instrument to pass through the spool's opening. You should also have a poster board or white fabric, and a can of spray paint and a bottle of white glue or spray fixative.

Form a tight circle, shoulder to shoulder. Begin the game by inserting the nail or dowel through the spool so it rolls easily. Ask one person to hold the end of the thread, and hand the spool with the dowel through it to someone with whom one shares some element in common. Perhaps two have children on the same soccer team, both have degrees in English, or are wearing the same colors.

After a connection is made, ask the second person to loop the spool of thread around her or his index finger to form a point of tension. Be sure not to pull the thread or string too tightly and do not loop the thread all the way around your finger, just around the outside. Then pass the spool to someone else, explaining your specific connection with that person to the group. The spool will unroll easily, using the dowel to pass the thread. Continue passing

1 London and Recio, *Sacred Rituals: Connecting With Spirit Through Labyrinths, Sand Paintings and Other Traditional Arts*, is one of a number of books that offers ideas.

the spool until a tapestry forms of your entire group connections. Be creative and think of as many commonalities as you can, criss-crossing until your group thread sculpture resembles points of a star with a mass of thread lines.

When you are finished (or have run out of thread!), look at your group's creation and express any feelings, thoughts or insights gleaned from forming the thread sculpture.

To save your creation, you can lay it on a poster board or cloth and spray the entire surface with two or three colors of spray paint; when the paint is dry, remove the thread. You will have your creation in permanent form. Or you can apply the thread/string to the poster board with glue or spray fixative. Then the whole group can spray or brush paint the group's creation.

One group of five discovered that their thread sculpture formed a five-pointed star, which they mounted on card stock in a pentagon circle. The leader prepared a small color copy of it for each member to use as a bookmark. Some of them chose to glue or tie small symbolic items in the center to form a "dream catcher." Another group used the painted cloth to cover a small table they kept in the center of their dream circle, which served as a dream altar[1]. You are now ready to close until your next meeting

1 A dream altar is simply a small table that anchors the center of the dream circle's space. On dream retreats, the altar is created over several days as people spontaneously add meaningful items. When dream groups meet regularly, members can bring items to honor dreams they plan to share.

True/False Test

Take the following True/False test as a group. Discuss your answers and come to a consensus, so that you answer the questions together.

After you take the test, go over the answers and explanations together.

1. On occasion, dreams don't mean anything.
2. If you are on medication, it is one of the few times it is better to ignore the wild images that may appear in your dreams.
3. Eating spicy foods before going to sleep may affect dreams, and therefore their meaning.
4. When you dream about something from the day or two before (e.g., you have just been to a birthday party and then dream of one), the image doesn't have great significance.
5. In fact, most dreams are chiefly echoes of our daily activities, coming from the vast repository of our memory bank.
6. Dreams often are wish fulfillment.
7. Most dreams, when discussed in depth, end up usually being about sex.
8. Dreams don't predict the future.

9. Dictionaries of symbols are invaluable for understanding dream images.
10. Nightmares are indications of an unhealthy or deeply disturbed person.
11. Dreams are mostly “made up” from our fears and anxieties.
12. Spiritualized dream interpretations are popular in New Age circles, but they are usually incorrect.
13. One should endeavor to recall as many dreams as possible, because not remembering them means something is gravely wrong.
14. If you dream sexually about a person, it means you really have feelings of attraction you don’t want to face.
15. People who are good at dreams usually know what they mean when they wake up.
16. It’s ideal to understand the meaning of basic symbols, so when you dream about an image (e.g. flying means being ungrounded), you know what it means.
17. Silly, weird and embarrassing dreams are probably better ignored, especially if they are extremely ridiculous.
18. Waking life events are usually not related to the meaning of dreams.
19. Dreams rarely reveal information we don’t actually know.
20. After understanding the basic structure of dreams and their symbols, dreams are truly quite easy to understand.
21. People make the mistake of seeing too much meaning in dreams.
22. Unfortunately, it takes an expert to tell you what your dream really means.

The answer to each of the questions is: False.

1. Dreams always mean something; however, the dream's meaning is often elusive. A favorite defense of the ego is to declare a dream meaningless, but it is only the limited state of our mostly blind ego that can't get to the meaning. Don't fall for that trap. It is okay to say, "I don't know what this dream means." Sometimes the meaning will come years after the dream arrives.

2. & 3. Medications and spicy foods may affect dreaming, but to ignore the dreams that come during those times would be like going on a fasting vision quest only to ignore the dreams inspired by the quest. Medications can and will encourage colorful or powerful dreams. These dreams are especially important to track, because they may come from a deeper layer of the psyche.

4. There are trillions of memories, fantasies, thoughts, feelings and experiences from which a dream may have been drawn, so every specific dream image has a significant association. You have to ask why the dream-maker selected those particular images for your nighttime drama.

5. I think a person who begins to look at dreams from an open-minded perspective will see that dreams are more than a replay of our daily activities. Again, you have to be curious and ask, "Why this image, why this memory, or why this event?" Try to achieve open-minded scientific thinking, and be willing to take in new data, not merely search for reasons to confirm your set perceptions.

6. To say that a dream is wish fulfillment is to ascribe to the dream-maker the attitude of the ego. The author of our dreams is autonomous, quite independent from our waking ego. That is, the dream-maker is trying to inform the ego, not provide information of which the ego is well aware. Why would we dream of something we already know? A common confusion here is to say, "Yes, but I dreamed about a beautiful girl who was flirting with me, and I

know it's just because I wish I had a girlfriend like that." What the dreamer is ignoring is that the beautiful girl is a part of himself that wants attention and integration. Knowing that the dream image is significant provides a much richer and ultimately more useful way to approach dream material. The preconception that dreams are wish fulfillment denotes a type of shame, and is a clever way the ego defends against the true impact of the dream. Do not feel shame about any dream material, no matter how embarrassing it may seem at first.

7. Some dreams actually are about sex, but most are not. They are about spirituality, creativity, love, growth, development, physical illness or anything else we can imagine. Sex plays a part in dreams when that is made clear by the dreamer' associations.

8. Some dreams do indicate future trends – like a weather forecast or an arrow pointing in a certain direction. These are "prospective" dreams, dreams that carry a forecast. Dreams that actually do predict literal events are hard to differentiate from purely symbolic dreams. That is why it is helpful to date and record dreams thoroughly, to discern what is actually dreamed about ahead of time; then you might, over a period of time, begin to ascertain which dreams feel like they may be predictive.

9. Dictionaries of symbols eliminate the important step of hearing the dreamer's associations to images, which is the quintessential process in understanding dreams. Only in the most puzzling cases should the symbol dictionary be consulted.

10. Nightmares are actually gifts from the spirit world, strong messages that something needs attention: your painful past, your marriage relationship or your last job. Nightmares are correctives given in a spirit of concern.

11. Dreams can reflect true fear and anxiety. Usually, if you have a dream that tends to suggest anxiety, there is more anxiety than

your waking ego is able to acknowledge. This is helpful information, because it tells you what is really going on in your inner world.

12. Just as most dreams are not sexual, neither is the majority spiritual. That is not to say that dreams are never spiritual. Dreams can be about anything, and it is up to the investigators in a dream group to try to tease out their specific nuances.

13. Quite the contrary, whatever you remember is just right. Try not to judge your dreams, their content, length or how often you remember them. If you simply cannot remember any dreams at all, or would like to remember them more clearly, try this foolproof method; begin by finding a journal that you really like, one that "speaks to you." Put it by your bed with a nice pen, all ready for recording your dreams. Without fail, when first you wake, record the date in your journal and any thoughts, feelings, vague images or total nothingness you recall. Keep doing this for several days, *not skipping any days at all.* Record whatever you awaken with, no matter how small or insignificant it seems. You might record, "No dream whatsoever." The next morning you might record, "Only a vague feeling of unease." The third morning you might record, "A fragment of an image: I saw a small girl. That was all." Within a few nights, you will remember an entire dream. Think of it as fishing. At first, you may get only a nibble, and it takes a bit of patience to catch a fish. But it is very foolish to ignore a nibble, even a small one.

14. Dreaming that you have a sexual attraction to any individual certainly can indicate sexual feelings that are unconscious, but often this dream is about wanting to integrate a part of oneself that has been projected onto the sexy character in the dream.

15. I find that people who gain the most from their dream work usually admit that dreams are quite puzzling, and they have no idea what they mean until they are worked. Understanding dreams

requires an attitude of humility from the ego. Knowing may not be knowing.

16. As stated earlier, making personal associations is imperative in working with dreams (as we will see in the next chapter).

17. Often, the dreams that bring the most insights are the ones we want to forget, ignore, discount, or edit.

18. Waking life events are extremely important in dream work. This is called the waking context of a dream. Certainly, fighting breast cancer, looking for work, or finishing college are all life events that would be important factors to consider in a dream's meaning.

19. Dreams almost always present information we don't already know – ergo the dream. Even if we "know" something already, the dream presents a new take on it or a new emphasis. It is helpful to ask, "What is the new information this dream presents?" I might dream about being anxious, and determine that this is about an upcoming exam. I think, "Well, I already knew I was anxious," but among other things, the dream might be suggesting that the dreamer is more anxious than his or her ego has realized. Dreams come from an unconscious place in the psyche; it would not be a dream if we already knew it.

20. A dream can remain a mystery for years and years. Some are a bit obvious, but almost all of them are difficult to understand.

21. Actually, most people make the mistake of not paying nearly enough attention to their dreams.

22. Only the dreamer can say, ultimately, what his or her dream means or doesn't mean.

Homework

For the next session, bring pictures from newspapers, magazines or the Internet that evoke feelings.

Associations

Materials needed: magazine and/or newspaper photos that evoke feelings.

Learning to associate to imagery is essential to understanding dreams. Unless you develop this skill, dream work will be frustrating and will forever remain an enigma. The following exercise will sharpen your ability to work with the kinds of images that appear in dreams. For this meeting, the group needs several pictures that evoke emotional responses. Pictures from magazines of animals, landscapes, action shots or famous people will be fine for the exercise.

Making associations is the art of reaching into a repository of memory, opinion, thought and feeling in response to an image. When you look at an image, say whatever comes to mind. Don't censor your response, even if it is embarrassing. Just let it flow. Open the valve, take a deep breath and leap into the inner self. Sometimes I tell people to double click on the image and pull up your personal file.

If you want a way to begin you can start by using terms from typology.[1]

1 Myers, *Gifts Differing*; Jung, *Psychological Types, C.W. Vol. 6,* and von Franz and Hillman, *Jung's Typology* are very helpful sources on typology.

1. What is this object called? A tree – Thinking.
2. What is it? A large living plant, usually with leaves and roots, bark and branches – Sensation.
3. How do you feel about it? I love trees – Feeling.
4. What does the tree mean to you in a larger context? Trees are life and earth for me (or my tree of life) – Intuition.

Let's take the example of a picture of an icy, snowy landscape – a frozen lake, snow-covered trees and a grey sky. The first person to respond might say something like this:

"I feel cold when I look at this picture; it is white and sterile. It reminds me of Canada where I nearly froze to death the winter my family had to live there for my dad's job. We came back after six months, and I have never been so glad to be warm. But I loved Canada and still miss it. I was always cold then, but I have some wistful memories about those months. My parents still got along then."

Or someone might say:

"I love to ski, and this image makes me want to call a travel agent as soon as possible. Skiing makes me feel free, like I am flying, and I certainly am not getting enough of that these days."

Or:

"I think I am frozen inside. Just like this picture, I seem to have no feelings even though I know I must. I am cold from the inside out."

EXERCISE

Part One

Ask one person to select a picture and show it to the group. Place it in a location where everyone can see it, and let each person take a turn making associations to the image. While each individual associates, everyone else should listen attentively, but with no discussion. Simply let each group member openly and freely associate to the same image. The challenge here is not simply to repeat what others have said. Try to make your associations as personal as possible. Even though you may have a reaction or opinion similar to others in your group, no one has lived your life or had your unique experiences. Use the photos to access *personal* memories. Then repeat the exercise with a different picture.

After everyone has finished making associations to the images, talk about how this exercise felt. Did it feel difficult? Silly? Easy? Embarrassing? Talk about all of the feelings in the group, no matter how trivial, personal, awkward or pointless they may have seemed.

Did one person's association evoke another's? Was it difficult not to repeat each other? Did anyone experience blocking, where nothing would come to mind?

Part Two

Now select a partner, and in groups of two, take turns associating to random images again. You may want to scatter about the room so you have a little quiet space to focus on this exercise.

As an empathic listener you can make encouraging comments like "Go on," or "Tell me more about that." It is important that you not invade privacy or pry into sensitive issues; just encourage your partner to continue making associations. Take turns playing the role of encouraging listener and notice whether having an empathic listener makes it easier to associate to the images.

"When I look at this doll, broken and lying in the alley, I feel sad."

" – Anything else?"

"No, not really." Silence.

"Does this picture remind you of anything?"

"No."

"Where do you think this alley is?"

"Well, I think this is Turkey."

"Turkey?"

"Yes, I have always heard about their folk dolls, and this looks like one. Probably there was an earthquake there, and this is the destruction left from that disaster. Always, good things are damaged beyond repair when a big event like that happens."

In this case, the listener had to work a bit to get her partner to open up. Another acceptable question in this exercise is: "What if you made up a story about this picture?"

Next, take your listening skills a step farther by noticing the emotional punctuation in your partner's associations to a new image. Where does the energy reveal itself in the associations? Where might italics or exclamation points be? You may have to listen longer than you'd expect to hear the "click," but your patience will be rewarded. Let silence hang in the air past your usual comfort level. Simply wait for the person doing the associating to drop into thoughts, feelings, and memories, speaking up only to encourage the associations. When the exchange seems complete, say what you have heard, and ask the person associating to confirm or deny that you understood what was said.

For example, the listener might say, "I heard 'frozen' used as a metaphor for no feelings." "I heard energy around skiing and the desire for more freedom." "I heard memories about living in Canada that seemed bittersweet, and some issues about growing up in a family where parents fought a lot." "I heard sadness around lost innocence as a result of destruction." And most important, "Is that accurate?"

Here are some examples of comments that would *not* be appropriate:

"I think you need to work on old issues about your parents and family of origin stuff."

"It seems like you are really a frozen person. You have a cold way about you."

"I think you need to get more freedom in your life; probably it is a marriage problem."

"I think you are blocking a painful memory in this alley picture because I had to push you to say anything."

Judgmental comments make the person doing the associating defensive for being vulnerable and honest; they do not engender openness or trust. That is why it is especially important for the person who makes the associations to confirm or deny that the listener heard correctly. "Yes, that is how I felt." Or, "No, that is not really what the image brought up in me. It was more about the feeling of nostalgia." Empathetic listeners mirror, re-state and re-frame what they have heard in tentative, not declarative language. They ask questions such as "Is it possible that you are feeling … .?" rather than declaring "You are feeling … ." They create an empathic circle in which trust can develop.

As each partner takes a turn associating, the listener practices hearing the italics, the emphasis or the "Oomph!" the image brings forth; the one associating confirms or denies whether the listener heard correctly. This dance back and forth, back and forth, is like kneading bread dough. At some point, the dough will be perfect – satiny smooth and ready to rest under the towel.

Take a short break, and then regroup into the full circle to share your experiences. How did your exchange of associations go? Was it fun? Confusing? Do you need to practice more? What came up emotionally or psychologically from the pictures that you selected?

Part Three

Repeat this associative process in the larger group, using dream material for the associations rather than images from magazines. Ask one person to tell a dream image (not a whole dream) to the group, then encourage and coax the dreamer to make associations to the dream image. Again, obtain confirmation from the dreamer that the associations have been heard correctly. Here is an example:

"I dreamed I looked in the mirror and saw I had terrible acne."

"Do you have an association to acne?"

"I find it embarrassing and shameful. I guess my mother felt that way, and I do too."

"It sounds like your association is to shame, seeing something about yourself that is embarrassing?"

"Yes, that feels right."

Do not interpret the dream, do not offer advice and do not suggest how the dreamer feels.

After one dream image has been fully explored, let another member take a turn. Do not expect the process to go quickly. Continue sharing dream images and making associations to the dream images until everyone has had a turn.

Exercise

Divide into two's or three's. Each person takes three items out of his/her pocket/purse and puts them in a pile together with other members' items. Then, using a rule, divide the items into two groups. An example of a rule would be: items that contain metal and items that don't contain metal. Record the rule. Regroup the items and divide again, using another rule. Do this as many times as you can; keep going even after you think you have thought of everything. When all lines of thought are exhausted, get back into the larger group and share your rules.

This is an exercise I taught to sixth graders in a gifted science program a number of years ago. The goal is to teach classification. A thorough scientist can make sixty observations just from looking at a burning candle. The point of this exercise is to see how dream images, aspects, feelings and themes can all be categorized in groupings of endless possibilities. When associating to dream images, you will gain from opening your mind to all those possibilities. Here are some ideas to help you get started:

Items that contain writing, and those that don't.

Items that involve the government or don't.

Items that are natural and those that aren't.

Items that are tools and those that aren't.

Items that have belonged to someone else, and those that haven't.

Items that are consumable and those that aren't.

Items that dissolve in water and those that don't.

Items that contain numbers and those that don't.

All-black items and those that aren't black.

All items invented before 1500 and those that are invented afterward.

Etc.

Process the experience you had in this exercise. Did you feel clever, slow, or perhaps creative? Did others' rules provoke some of your own? Did you want this exercise to stop, or to go on? Is there any value to this exercise, and if so what is it? What could this have to do with dream associations?

Part Two

Foundations

photo: Shelly Deh

Delineating the Structure of Dreams

Dreams can be puzzling, long, complex and hard to understand. As with any difficult task, whether finishing a Ph.D. dissertation or having a sit-down Thanksgiving dinner for thirty people, it is helpful to divide the task or dream into manageable pieces that are much easier to digest. Analyzing a dream is easier if accomplished one step at a time.

Making associations to dream images is the first and most important step in gathering the information you need about your dream. Associations provide a detailed, zoom-in picture, like picking up a rock on your hike in the mountains and studying it because you have been drawn to it. But then, what is one to do with all of this associated material? After associations are made, the next step is looking at the basic framework of the dream for the big picture, like going to the top of Mt. Evans and looking at the entire view of the Rocky Mountains in Colorado.

So let's practice the art of clarifying a dream by studying its elements and then analyzing its structure. For now, let's define structure as containing the following elements:

Title
Plot
Character
Setting
Feelings/ Mood

Main Idea or Author's Message

It is helpful to see an example in which a dream's structure is broken up into the parts outlined above. The following dream provides a prototype that will help your circle understand how structure is delineated . Furthermore, this dream is one that will be referred to later in the handbook, because it falls into the category of "A dream everyone can benefit from hearing."

Title

To begin, title your dream. Titles reflect a salient idea, theme or the general sense of a work. The best are usually simple, short and to the point. Titling your dream already begins to frame and contain the dream. The following dream is entitled "Dancing on the Graves":

> *I dreamed I was walking or trudging up a hill in Boulder, Colorado, by the campus of the University of Colorado. I saw the city cemetery and decided to go in. As I entered, it seemed to get bigger, and I realized it became the cemetery of the whole world. The grave markers went on and on over hills as far as I could see. Then I started to step on the burial mounds – one step for each body buried. They were closer together than I had seen before, really packed in tightly, with no space between each plot. As I stepped on each person's grassy space, I was aware that this was taboo. Didn't I remember as a child being told it was bad luck to step on a grave in a cemetery? But I continued, and gathered momentum to the point that it seemed like a rhythm developed, one step, one beat, one step, one beat, until a dance erupted and I danced and danced with complete freedom and abandon. I awakened suddenly from this dream with a jolt and an acute awareness: no one can enter this sacred place, where all of the people who have ever lived and died on earth from the beginning of time are buried, and not see the point. All life ends sooner or later, and the only response to the puzzling human dilemma is to dance.*

Plot

What is the action in the dream? To outline the plot, simply state what happens in the dream and in what order. Describe the action with facts alone. Just as in analyzing a play, book or movie, we want to know what took place. The plot of "Dancing on the Graves" is that the dreamer walks up a hill near the University of Colorado campus. He enters a cemetery. He walks and then dances on the graves.

A clearly stated plot carves away all the material from the dream except the specific action that occurred. Already, this dream seems more manageable.

Character

For every dream, list all of the characters who appear, their ages and anything well-defined about them; then determine from whose point of view the images are observed. "Dancing on the Graves" has only one character: the dream ego. The dream ego is the person whose eyes we are looking through during the dream. If you are a cat in your dream, then the dream ego is a cat. Like the point of view of a character in a story or novel, the dream ego determines how we see the images in a dream. We see the events as the dream ego experiences them.

Sometimes the dream ego doesn't appear in a dream, and action is observed objectively, as if by a camera. In that case, there could certainly be a list of characters; only the dreamer would not appear. If the "Dancing on the Graves" dream were a short play or film, only one actor would be listed. Complete your work on the characters in your dream by making associations to all those who appear in it, just as you have practiced associating to other images. Be sure to include how old each character is in your dream, including the dream ego. The dream ego in "Dancing on the Graves" was thirty years old.

Setting

What time of day is it? What time of year? What is the weather? And of course, vitally important, what is the setting? The setting of "Dancing on the Graves" is Boulder Colorado, "The Hill" just below the city cemetery, which becomes a vast cemetery of all who have lived and died. The time of day is mid-day, the weather is Colorado sunny, and it seems like summer since the grass is green. The setting may be real or fictitious or contain elements of both.

Feelings, Mood

Attention to the affective tone, the feelings and mood of the dream, is crucial. A dream group might hear two dreams that are quite similar in plot and setting, but if the feelings in the dreams are quite different, then the dreams indicate entirely different inner situations. It is quite possible to dream that a loved one has died and yet not feel terribly sad in the dream. It is also possible to dream about something rather uneventful, such as walking in mud and having it stick to your shoes, and find that the dream carries a powerful emotion such as terror or shame. Think of feeling (is something good or bad?) as an evaluation of a dream image. It also contains emotion based on the opinion of the dream-maker. Films often tell us the feeling and emotion in a scene with the music in the background. By the music we know if something is going to jump out of the closet as our protagonist approaches. The musical score can communicate love, sadness, fear, hope and so on. It is critical to understand what musical score would go with your dream, what emotion is evoked. Therefore, take extra time to go back into your dream; note how you felt during the dream and how you feel now about events in the dream.

In "Dancing on the Graves" the feelings are very powerful. At first, the dream ego felt curiosity, then awe (a numinous feeling) and, finally, the breathtaking sense of receiving a life-altering message.

Main Idea or Author's Message

After the elements of a dream have been identified, described and amplified with the dreamer's associations, we can begin to speculate about the implications of the dream. It is possible that you will not yet have an answer to the question of the dream's meaning. Perhaps it won't ever come. Meaning is not necessarily the most important part of dream work. Many times, simply sitting with the images and feelings is quite enough. But some dreams, such as "Dancing on the Graves," come with a sense of an understanding, or epiphany, that is trying to break through to consciousness. To discover the "author's message," you could ask yourself, "What is this dream trying to tell me?" or "How am I being confronted in this dream?" or "What is the good news or bad news in this dream? or "What in this dream is new information?"

The main thrust of "Dancing on the Graves" was clear to the dreamer as soon as he awakened. Like Dante approaching the gates to the underworld in The Divine Comedy[1], he was struck by the vast numbers of people who have lived and died. When he entered the cemetery, it became for him "the cemetery of the whole world," and the "grave markers went on and on over hills as far as [he] could see." Aware of the vast numbers of the dead, he realized that "no one can enter this sacred space where all of the people who have ever lived and died on earth from the beginning of time are buried and not see the point – that the only response to this puzzling human dilemma is to dance." The dreamer described himself as a young man who had "an anxious, driven, possessed ego" which was regularly taken over by a competitive, cold, critical complex. He badly needed to hear the dream's confrontation, to make his life more playful, spontaneous, joyful and outrageous.

1 Ciardi (Translator), *The Divine Comedy by Dante Alighieri*

Exercise

Select a dream that your circle can use for practice in defining the elements and structure of a dream. For now, refrain from dream interpretation, or "understanding" the dream; you may leave "Author's Message" blank for now if you don't know what your dream might be revealing. Then let each person take a turn until everyone has had a chance to have a dream clarified by the process of defining and analyzing its elements. Often, sharing aloud in a group helps insights emerge, and writing them down is also helpful. Some people include notes in this step in their dream journals. Each dreamer can record her or his structure while the whole group helps with the process of defining and clarifying the elements of each dream. The circle's role in this case is to assist, not to interject one's own thoughts about what a person's setting, tone, meaning – or anything else – might be. This process could take several sessions. Please allow the work to be unhurried and methodical, since this is how dreams come alive.

The Literature of Dreams

Perhaps dreams are our original storytellers, the beginning of image, fiction, poetry, myth, drama and plot. Films seem to be somewhat like dreams, but novels are too, as well as many pieces of art. Dreams are so multi-faceted and dense that all of our art forms seem fueled by dream material, yet still only hint at a measure of the impact a dream can make on a dreamer. A specific lens through which to view your dream is the perspective of literature. Here one finds hyperbole, metaphor, foreshadowing, punning and irony[1].

Hyperbole is exaggeration: the clown's bulbous red nose, his shoes the size of skate-boards and his baggy pants with giant polka dots are all exaggerated images that are hyperbolical. This is a cornerstone of humor, but it factors into nightmares, too. (Frightening images that are loud, overdrawn and shocking will be discussed in a later chapter.) In dreams, the image is often overstated so that the dreamer can discover the confrontation. There might be endless empty rooms in the dream house, or the kitchen could be teeming with ants; these pictures evoke strong emotional reactions that serve as an alarm clock or a cheering section, depending on the dream's point. To waylay the waking self, well shielded in a cloak of "I don't care, it doesn't matter, that's silly, stupid, or too scary to think about," the dream-maker has to take extraordinary measures.

---

1 A good reference source: Cuddon, *The Penguin Dictionary of Literary Terms and Literary Theory* (see Bibliography)

In discovering associations, it becomes apparent that dreams are filled with metaphorical images. These are images that are actually representing something other than themselves. Painting a house white in a dream is not about painting a house white, it is a metaphor for something else. But what? We would have to ask the dreamer for clarification on the symbol; his associations are indispensable. Metaphor is the dream's language, one that has to be decoded through reflection.

Foreshadowing is a hint of what is to come. Again, in a similar way, background music in films lets us know that something bad is about to happen. Authors will prefigure tragedy by preparing us with a mini-tragedy as a clue to what happens later. In the film *Zorba the Greek*,[1] a woman in the small Greek village is attractive and haughty, and the men there both desire her and despise her. Her goat is killed early in the film, building tension and a sense of impending doom. It is difficult, later, to watch the scene in which the young, beautiful woman meets in the same fate.

Puns are ubiquitous in dreams. Every time a dream has in it an image or important word that has more than one meaning, I play with the possibility that there is a coded message as well as the one that's more obvious. When I was training in Zurich in the 1980s, we all joked about dreaming of our good friend, Battle Bell. Early on, someone pointed out that when Battle showed up in a dream, it indicated a battle was about to happen or was already happening or could happen. Battle was such a loveable, kind soul it was always humorous when this occurred, but then puns are a type of humor, however poor their reputation has become.[2] (Sadly, Battle Bell died in June 2006.)

Irony, too, is a sardonic flavor that dreams employ, just as art does. There is irony in dreaming that a political figure you may despise is a dear lover, or that the answer to the mystery of life is

1 "Zorba The Greek," M. Cacoyannis, Dir., 20th Century Fox, 1964
2 Fitzpatrick, "On The Passing of Battle Bell"

told to you, only to find you cannot remember it in the morning. Dreams are filled with biting wit, paradoxical plot lines and shocking conclusions, all a surprise to the ego – as is irony.

This is only a first look at the overlap between dreams and art forms. You may want to add to this list over time.

EXERCISE

Using dreams from the dream circle, give the group time to find examples that illustrate hyperbole, punning, foreshadowing, metaphor and irony. You may want to look at a particular dream as if it were a film, selecting the tone and camera angles, and casting the leads and supporting characters to amplify irony, foreshadowing and other literary devices. Share together how this exercise changes your sense of dreams, or how it might frustrate you, excite you, broaden your understanding or increase your respect for dreams.

The Waking Context

There is one more vital step in beginning to understand the mysteries dreams can hold; we need to factor in the waking context. What does this mean? Quite simply, to explore the life issues and events that occurred in your waking life around the time you had your dream. Let's go back to the acne dream. The dreamer, you recall, looked in her mirror, saw that she had acne, and was ashamed. One question to ask her would be, "Is there anything in your waking life that you are feeling embarrassed about?" She might answer, "Oh, yes – I think I know what this is about. I was very bratty on our trip to Italy last month. I was really rude to some people on the tour and didn't even know why I was acting so badly. I had the dream just as we came home. I guess I'm seeing a part of myself that is not attractive and that I am somewhat ashamed of." If the group has developed enough trust by this point, it would be all right to ask the dreamer, "Any idea what part of yourself this could be?" The dreamer might say, "Well, I was jealous of the people on the tour who seemed so rich and had it so easy. They were young, and everything was paid for, no budgeting needed at all. I was really irritated that my children don't have that advantage. I guess I'm more materialistic than I like to admit to myself."

The waking context can include significant issues such as illness, a cross-country move, the death of a friend, or smaller matters like a recent temper tantrum at the bank. *Within our associations, we need to relate our dream images to current events.* Often, dream images will refer us back to earlier events that seemed totally meaningless at the time, but in fact hold the key to understanding those images.

The waking context takes time to explore in dream group. It requires respect, trust, confidentiality and total commitment from each person. It also calls for a non-judgmental attitude. In such an environment of trust in workshops and seminars, I have found people willing to become vulnerable over the course of only a couple of hours. Transgender issues, drug abuse, tax evasion and other delicate topics can quickly become important when discussing the waking context of a dream. I do not advise you to join a dream group unless you are willing to be open and frank about your life issues. If not, your dream work will be stilted, dry and devoid of the full range of discovery that openness allows.

Exercise

Practice with a couple of dreams in your group. As before, make associations to images and delineate the structure of the dream, but now add the waking context to the discussion. Be sure that only the dreamers say what their dreams now reveal. How do those dreamers feel? Was this exploration helpful? Were the other group members kind and supportive in their questions? Keep working with the dreams, carefully examining them until your session time is over, always being aware not to grab for meaning, but letting the imagery and associations speak for themselves.

To Make Meaning, Explore Images, Find Guidance

As stated earlier, it is tempting for the ego, the conscious waking self, to grasp at meaning, to draw conclusions too quickly about dream material. Some common dream "interpretations," such as, "If I dream of black crows, someone will die by the end of the week," are obviously ridiculous. Nonsensical answers like that are found in most dream dictionaries. This formulistic reasoning can seem logical and real even to the dreamer, but it is, in any literal sense, rarely accurate. For example, having a sexual encounter with someone in a dream does not generally mean that you are about to have an affair with that, or any other person.

Ironically, the first step in understanding dreams is to know that you probably do not understand dreams, especially the one you are currently exploring. Jung once remarked, "Presented with a dream, the first thing I tell myself is, 'I have no idea what this dream means.'"[1] We are soon humbled by the dream-maker; we truly don't know just what our dream is revealing, otherwise, we wouldn't have had that dream. Dreams are material straight from the unconscious. After associations are made to all of the dream images, after the waking context is discussed and the feelings are explored, the salient question is: "What information does this dream provide that the dreamer didn't already know?"

So, now we know that we don't know anything, what next?

---

1 Jung, "On the Nature of Dreams," *Collected Works*, Vol. 8, par. 533

First, let's recognize that some dreams are far more transparent than others. Some dreams, "Dancing on the Graves," for example, come with their meaning rather clearly stated. Other dreams, however, take years to explore, to sift through, to savor and digest before they begin to reveal their meaning.

Let's look at "meaning" for a moment. What is it really? When we go to an art gallery, do we need the paintings and sculptures to mean something? Or rather, are we there to experience something? Art can provoke emotion, it can serve as a vehicle to new ways of seeing, it can cause a shift in consciousness, or it can inspire. Meaning is probably not the principal reason we gaze at art, attend the ballet or listen to music, and dreams are very like works of art. Some of them only suggest an experience, but offer an invitation to feel differently about an important aspect of life.

Pushing for meaning is a tendency that will hinder valuable experiences with dreams, and will influence their impact. Meaning simply arrives at the door of the ego quite unexpectedly. It may seem as if a light is suddenly turned on, or it may seep into consciousness like drip irrigation in a garden. It cannot be predicted or forced.

In fact, the compulsion to find meaning is exactly what you need to let go of in order for meaning to emerge. It is, however, useful to focus on feelings, associations and the waking context. If the dream stumps the dreamer, then the dough needs to sit under the towel a while longer. Speculating about meaning at an early stage of considering a dream may cause the dreamer to miss the nibbles she is trying to snag on the fishing line. Others' thoughts may chase hers away. After enough time, and if the dreamer requests it, the group may make suggestions (like a multiple choice exam) that she can confirm or deny based on her instincts. But even then, it is absolutely essential for the group to support primarily the dreamer's thoughts, feelings and conclusions about her dream.

Even if you are almost certain that you have the inside track on a person's dream, keep your mouth shut. Harsh as that may sound, it might be the single most important ingredient in the dream group stew. Without respect for the dreamer's ability to determine the dream's message for himself, there will not be a dream group. People will become too busy to attend; new jobs, relationships, or something else will interfere, because meaning is not really very important in working with dreams. Freedom and trust within the group to explore freely is what is important, because that's what allows people to transform. There are no exceptions. Never, under any circumstances, is it appropriate to tell another person what her dream means or what she should do. Even if you are absolutely sure you know just what someone else's dream means, it won't result in any awareness or change unless the dreamer discovers it herself. This takes a lot of self control. In the rush and excitement that dreams can generate, that rule can sometimes be forgotten. The dreamer, however, will know in some visceral way that her boundaries have been violated. Always let the dreamer say if she wants any suggestions, and then ask whether the suggestions offered feel right to her.

In a family dream group, this is especially important for children. Children are not on the same level as their parents in the waking world. But in the dream world, it is an entirely different matter. Here all parties are equal, and no parent can tell a child what a dream is suggesting any more than a child can interpret a parent's dream. Personal respect is essential.

Sometimes dream group members are strangers at first, and it is quite a task to reveal personal, vulnerable material to people we don't even know, much less trust. The rule of allowing only the dreamer to say what the dream means will build trust in a group. If I know I can say anything about myself and my dream and no one will contradict me, I am much more likely to get down to the raw, grimy stuff of my psyche. We need to be given a safe opportunity to explore ourselves, not a tyrannical attitude that pushes and prods.

A key issue here is privacy. Some people will not be able to reveal many of the most important issues in their lives for months, or even years after a dream group begins. It is the degree to which the group is non-judgmental and non-directive that will determine how deep the trust and sharing will become among the members. Some groups share their most intimate issues and experiences, and others remain superficial. The more open each member is, and the more respectful each is of the other, the deeper the group and the dreams will go.

So is meaning possible in dream groups, and if so, how can it be encouraged? It is entirely possible to encourage consciousness and awareness and direction and meaning from dreams. The process is something like connecting the dots of a puzzle that has to be solved. Players need only draw lines in sequence in order to bring form to chaos. Dreams, as puzzles, are quite the same: we look at images, we trace a plot, we consider emotions, we factor in waking events, and sometimes we have an insight.

Here is a dream:

> *I am by a rushing river and see a small girl floundering in the water. It is clear she is drowning. I grab her and see she has terribly thin arms and is malnourished. She grabs me around the neck with her fragile arms and peers at me with large, brown, sad eyes. I awaken crying.*

So let's try our method on this dream:

Title: The Near Drowning

Plot: A girl is drowning and the dreamer rescues her.

Character: A girl child who is thin and sad, about three years old. The dream ego, a woman of forty-three.

Feelings: Profound compassion and empathy for the undernourished, endangered child.

Waking Context: The dreamer is an artist with some success who, nevertheless, neglects her art.

The meaning is not too obscure in this dream. It seems the artist/dreamer needed to develop her art because it was far more significant than she was pretending to herself. The dream corrected her cavalier attitude of, "Oh, I can work on my art later when I am not so busy, after my daughter graduates, after we finish moving into the new house, when my situation at work settles down, etc." The dream's content suggested that the dreamer's situation was critical and that the artistic self portrayed by the child was about to be lost to the river. The dream confronted the dreamer in such a way that she knew very quickly what it was about. She nodded, and said, "Oh yes, I am putting off and putting off doing any art right now, even though I am in the middle of an exciting piece. I have just left it alone for months." But please note that the dreamer, not the group, formed this conclusion.

Here is another dream:

> *I dream I am in a throne room. I see a great nude goddess in the front at a throne or altar. She is about ten feet tall. Next to me is the red devil. He is charming, and I realize I am on his side. We are throwing fire-balls at her.*

It was nearly impossible to extract any meaning from this dream. The dreamer titled the dream, listed its characters, associated to the images and discussed his waking life issues. Nowhere did this dream emerge as meaning anything. It remains a powerful set of images with which he still works, however. Having no previous knowledge of the red devil and its history, he studied that. He looked at the masculine and feminine images in the dream and pondered this dichotomy for some months. He was quite taken with his dream; it allowed him to enter a realm he had not known. He was also disturbed by the dream and wondered if he were in league with the devil, but nothing in his life indicated that. If we were to speculate at all, it could be noted that he had an agreeable personality, but perhaps was not really expressing his passion and personal power.

Remember, some dreams show their meaning easily, and others do not. It is neither necessary nor essential to always find meaning in dreams; groups who insist on finding meaning as the most significant point will usually fail.

EXERCISE

Try the following process in your group, to see if meaning will unfold. Ask someone to share a dream, preferably a recent dream, since older dreams have their own set of rules and parameters. Use all of the tools you have learned so far to uncover feelings, thoughts, associations, insights and meaning. Use the rules of literature and map out the structure. Now you can add one more step: look for the good news and the bad news the dream presents. This is another way to detect some meaning. Then, for each dream the group has worked with in the last several sessions, go back and see if the dreamer can voice the good news and the bad news, the "author's message," or some meaning in each dream.

Please keep in mind that only the dreamer – no one else – can state meaning, not even as a question. And by all means, *do not say, "If it were my dream it would mean ... ."* This is an indirect way to tell a person what his dream means, and in my experience it does not respect the dreamer's individual boundary. Much later in this guidebook, I will outline a process that permits dream group members to interact with one another's dream material in a way that protects both the integrity of the dream and the dreamer.

To Receive, Not Capture the Dream

An analyst friend, Henry Straw of Houston, Texas, used the metaphor long ago of catching a dream like a professional quarterback reaching for a long pass with gentle hands. This is the ideal way to deal with dreams in all cases, with all people, in all groups, at all times, and it may be the only rule for which there is no exception. Like a midwife who "catches" an infant, in contrast to the use of forceps in earlier obstetric practices, treat a dream as gently as a baby being born. Dreams are often a vulnerable new part of the self, and they have to be treated with the utmost care. Yes, even the most frightening or disgusting dreams.

Additionally, to receive a dream rather than capture it promotes a caring attitude for dream material, one's own as well as others'. Dreams are like letters. We need simply to open and read them. Dreams don't have to be hunted down, trapped, or shot. We do not want to end up with something lifeless. What we want is a living dream that still has emerging properties, properties that can develop over time.

As a dream matures, it may take on new and richer meanings or give additional direction. Reviewing dreams weeks, months, or even years later is quite an illuminating process. It must be that they continue to work, or "cook" over time because all the people I know who have practiced this discipline, including myself, have had the same experience. Dreams continue to manifest awareness long after we first encounter them.

I ask that you think of the dream as a living organism. It is in process, like a recently planted tree that may take years to be realized as its true magnificent self. Receiving, rather than capturing a dream, requires us to suspend dogmatic attitudes and the desire to find a quick result. Sometimes, dreams confuse us and we want to put them aside as soon as possible. But it is okay, even good, to let a dream be mysterious. It's healthy for the ego that thinks it knows everything, and simply cannot be outwitted by a dream, to encounter mysterious complexity. Receiving a dream takes courage, patience, kindness, tolerance and respect. Approached with such attitudes, the dream will eventually reveal itself, no matter how shy it may seem at the beginning.

Here is an example:

A forty-six year old woman shared the following dream with her dream group:

> *I am talking to my ex-husband and find out that he had a girlfriend I didn't know about. I guess we are still married in the dream. I am so shocked and horrified I wake up.*

Her dream group was curious about leftover feelings she might have toward her former husband. She didn't have any, she said. They argued with her. She argued back. The leader expressed dismay that she couldn't seem to admit that there might still be grief over, or pain in adjusting to, her divorce. She didn't agree. The leader (me!) was sure she was resisting her feelings about the former marriage.

The next week, the woman miscarried her first pregnancy, which she and her second husband had undergone arduous medical fertility procedures to accomplish. When she came back to dream group, she told us the dream had predicted her feelings that were to come. She was horrified and shocked by the end of her pregnancy. I concur with her conclusions completely. Occasionally, we are prepared by the dream-maker for events that will occur in our lives. Her dream portrayed quite accurately her feelings about her miscarriage, and the closest analogy was her divorce. The dream was not about her divorce; it was about the feeling of shock that was, unfortunately, yet to come.

This provides an example of just how mercurial dreams can be. It would have been virtually impossible for any group or dreamer to understand accurately the context of her dream the week before the difficult events unfolded. It would have been helpful, however, for the dreamer and group simply to collect the dream, the feelings, the images and the associations and to let it all rest. The dreamer was quite upset by her experience, and of course, our treatment of her dream did not help with her grief and trauma

This is why it is so important to allow those areas of dream work that seem either too messy, or too pat and obvious to remain open and unresolved. As stated, dreams may not fulfill their destiny or make themselves understood for many years, or they may become clear in a day or two. One is reminded of the statement Jung was reported to have made: "Dreams prepare the psyche for the events of the following day."[1]

Quite frequently, dreams will prepare us ahead of time for events about which we have no previous knowledge. However, dreams also discuss past events, as well as events that have never happened and never will happen. It is impossible to overstate how complex, diverse and intricate dreams are, how they can collapse shades of meaning into a single symbol and how they can adroitly comment on, humor and push us, all at the same time. They simply live in mystery in the transitional world, where mist and fog conceal precise understanding.

1 Private conversation with Jungian Analyst Mary Briner, 1986

"I Do Not Know" Exercise

Using a dream that has been found particularly perplexing, ask the dreamer to tell the dream, associate to all of the images in the dream, discuss the waking context, title the dream, and fully and completely explore all tributaries the dream leads the dreamer to discuss. Then have the dreamer say, "I have no idea what this dream means." Let each member say, "I have no idea what this dream means." Then the dreamer can say:

"I do not know what this dream means, but it makes me feel ..."

"I do not know what this dream means, but it reminds me of ..."

"I do not know what this dream means, but I am hoping it does not mean ..."

"I do not know what this dream means, but the dream might be about ..."

"I do not know what this dream means."

Try this exercise with several dreams. Then take time to discuss the experience of saying, "I don't know." Is it frustrating, freeing, foolish? Did any insights emerge about the dream material or your need to know what your dreams mean?

Dreams that do not readily reveal meaning can be inspirations for creative expression. Drawing a dream, painting a dream, making a collage out of tissue paper, magazines or other material, using clay or play dough to make a sculpture, writing a short story or an ending to the dream, using a musical instrument to compose a chord progression or melody that expresses the dream, or finding a piece of music to dance your dream are all ways to amplify dreams through creative expression.

Here's a challenge for each group meeting: leave at least one question on the table before you close. Let the unanswered question have a place in the dream group setting. And you who seek insight may balance yourselves by calling to mind the simple words, "I don't know."

Role-Play Exercise

For some comedy relief, try this role-play.

Using one volunteer to play a person sharing her dream, let the dream circle play being bad listeners. Give advice, use blanket "we" statements, be comforting and reassuring, declare interpretations and any other responses that could be discounting, demeaning and patronizing. Then process the exercise by hearing from the dreamer and the listeners about what each person felt during the exercise. The group can take turns being the dreamer.

Homework: Creative Dream Expression

Ask each member of the group to pick one of the earlier suggestions for creative expression (or think of another creative form); then, using a dream as inspiration, ask members to create a piece of art and bring it to the next meeting. If you think you know, for the most part, what your dreams mean, you can still benefit from this exercise. If you don't have your own dream, pick a dream you heard in the group that touched you in some way, and use that as your inspiration.

If the group prefers, it can use a group meeting to work on this activity together. The entire group can, for example, use clay, or each member could bring his or her own materials to the meeting. Take time to share with each other what you learned from this exercise, whether it was difficult, how you felt doing it, and what insights you feel you have uncovered.

Part Three

Depth

photo: Nicholas Frenc

To Fine Tune the Art of Listening to Dreams

Working with dreams is an art. Like any craft, it improves over time and takes years to develop fully. But for the necessary skills to develop, your dream circle must avoid the common and well-intentioned mistakes that could cause your dream group to fail.

The dream group process consists of three distinct and essential steps. Like listening to stories around a campfire, the first step in the dream circle is listening attentively to the entire dream as the dreamer relates it, and then asking the dreamer for associations to all of the dream images. We are curious, fascinated and desire to know everything the dreamer can tell us. Be careful to stay with the dream image, circumambulate it using associations rather than zigzagging away from the image down a rabbit hole of irrelevant material[1]. During this phase the group can help the dreamer delineate the structure of the dream as well as discuss the waking context. The focus in this step is on the dreamer, with no exceptions.

The next step is asking the dreamer to say what may be meaningful to him or her, what stands out or may be coming into some clarity after the discussion of the images in the dream. The dreamer is permitted, even encouraged to ramble freely and play with any ideas or feelings that may emerge. It certainly is acceptable to ask questions during this time, as long as they help the dreamer clarify his or her thoughts or feelings. Questions such as, "Are you feeling angry or sad about the scene with your sister?" Or, "Can you tell

1 See Jung, *Children's Dreams: Notes from the Seminar Given in 1936-1940*, p. 25

us what your relationship with your sister is right now?" are acceptable. The focus, however, remains on the dreamer and his or her associations, thoughts, feelings and conclusions.

In the third step, the group takes turns, and anyone who wants to may respond by saying how the dream touches her or him. Here the focus must shift to each group member's inner experience, not what the dream is expressing. Because of cultural mores, we are not always encouraged to think deeply about ourselves, so this step may not come easily. Moreover, judging others and projecting our own issues onto other people is second nature. It is all too natural to respond with statements such as, "This is what I think about your dream ...," "What I want you to hear in your dream is ...," "This is a really positive dream, because ...," or "Your dream is encouraging or warning you to ... ." To state any opinion about the dream or the dreamer's life is absolutely counter-productive, no matter how right or helpful you think your ideas are. It's not unusual to think we truly are helping when our actions are, in fact, rather toxic.

In a successful dream circle, the listeners need to respond to the dream from their own process, their own "resonance". Oddly enough, when listeners report only their feelings and associations to a dream, dreamers report feeling touched and heard, rather than labeled, bossed, controlled, or judged, as often happens when steps two and three are confused.

Dreams are windows to the unconscious. You want to know where the dreamer is going, so you must give that person your full and undivided attention. Then, when you make comments of any sort, they need to be fully and completely about your own process, without interpretation, conjecture or speculation.

Speak only for yourself. Instead of saying "We all feel the same way," a listener might say, "I identify with what she said because I have lived in the hard place of being a member of a minister's family. It's not an easy part of my life." Generalizations like, "We all need to be more independent," or "Women like us are always having problems with the men in our lives" stop the process of the dreamer, as well as that of the group. Such statements are a denial of both the dreamer's and the listener's individuality, and they are too judgmental.

Resisting the impulse to rush to interpretation or generalization, a listener might try saying something like, "Your dream really touched me, because my first husband [state your experience], but after we were divorced, I felt more … ." Odd though it seems, entirely personal comments will often open and broaden the dreamer's work, increase the listener's awareness and strengthen the group's trust[1].

Learning to focus on our own thoughts and feelings, however, is difficult, because it goes against so much of our training, our socialization and, often, our education. Consequently, many groups will encounter the following common pitfalls when well-intentioned members display tendencies to sublimate pain, to give advice, to over-generalize the dreamer's experience, to attempt to take care of the dreamer, or to avoid telling the truth. These ways of responding overlap and reinforce each other, compounding their negative effects.

1 One excellent way to highlight this point is with an exercise that helps members discover their associations to particular words (as well as to particular dream images): ask each member to take turns saying any word they like, and ask others to voice their associations to it. It is quickly apparent that members' individual associations arise from their differing memories and experiences, and it is equally true that hearing someone else's will quickly stimulate one's own association. "Fire," for example, triggers all sorts of associations, from sublime to tragic, depending on one's history. While one member might delight in the warmth, beauty and romance of fire, another's attention is riveted by the image of seeing her childhood house burn to the ground. The contrast between a simple association and the "click" or "Bong!" of deeper feeling often reveals valuable clues to a dream's meaning.

1. Sublimating Pain

Unfamiliar, difficult and painful material can be hard to contain. It's natural to want to rush in and make everything okay when someone is hurting. But sublimating the dreamer's pain is a common way for a dream's flow to be stopped. Redirecting pain by glorifying, romanticizing, dismissing, or rationalizing it is a denial of the dreamer's reality and interferes with the process of self-awareness. It is entirely possible that material will surface that is so painful that the circle will freeze; the pain has been avoided like a hot flame and the Work trying to emerge is lost.

For example, a dreamer might say, "I dreamed that I was in a very unfamiliar place that seemed burned out by a nuclear holocaust. I found parts of dead animals. There was a wounded dog that I think was dying, and I couldn't help it. I couldn't reach it."

A listener could respond by saying, "It sounds like it must have been very difficult."

The dreamer might continue with, "I can't reach out for the relationships I need. I think it may be about my mother. I feel as if there is something really burned up that I can't get to."

If the pain becomes too great, a group might fall into responses that look and sound like empathy, but actually deny or stop the process. For example, a listener might be tempted to say, "A lot of women have burned relationships, so I'm sure you'll be okay," which is like throwing water on a campfire. Or a circle member might try to give instruction: "Have you tried writing to your mother?" Worse yet would be to say, "Oh this is a good dream because … " Dreams are not good or bad, they simply *are*. It must be emphasized that attempts at encouragement, generalizations or giving advice may block the painful experience that needs to be faced and worked through. (More about giving advice will be addressed in the next section.)

Another way to stop a person's process dead in its tracks is to attempt to rescue by being too optimistic. "Oh, I think your mammogram will be fine." Or, "Have you tried talking directly to your neighbor about the conflict? I think if you just tried that, you would have a chance to express your displeasure and things could work out." As well-intentioned as these statements might be, they usually have at their core a need to ease or even suppress the listeners' discomfort. Spoken aloud, the message would be, "I want to rescue you, because listening to you makes me feel helpless, sad, and even terrified." That is why analysts and therapists are paid to listen; it is extremely hard work. The truth is, people suffer through difficult, painful experiences and die, and things are not always okay. Transformation comes only through the dreamer's work, not through rescue attempts.

If group members are uncomfortable with, or even unable to respond to this type of material, silence is a good option. When a dream circle can practice silence and know that it is a rich and important part of their time together, it can be enormously helpful. We are often trained to fill up silence with inane banter, encouragement and hand patting. Do your best to stretch yourselves to include the tension that silence produces; where there is tension, there is the possibility of resolution.

2. Giving Advice

One common response to a dream is, "If it were my dream ..." This can work to facilitate empathy and encourage the dreamer to be more open, but more often it is a subtly manipulative way of saying what a dream means, as well as a veiled attempt to tell the dreamer, "Here's what I think you should do, or feel, or think ... " For example, if I tell a dream about my husband taking over my art project, right away a group might start making statements like, "If it were my dream, I would tell my husband to stay out of my creative process." Or, "If it were my dream, I would be really angry at my husband." Pretty obvious, you may be thinking, whatever could be wrong with that?

What is wrong is that these responses project the feelings and perceptions of the listeners onto the dreamer. It is entirely possible that the dreamer has another reality, and needs to come to her or his own, different conclusions. In that case, the dreamer might say, "Well my husband is so creative, and I admire him so much – I think I let him carry the creative part of myself."

Here we have a subtle difference – not about judgment, not about anger or confrontation, but about the dreamer acknowledging a dynamic in her marriage and her unique process. Most important, she has taken responsibility for it. If a group member had said to her, "If it were my dream I would think that your creative husband is carrying your creative side," she might agree, but then she might not, because she didn't discover the information herself, it was spoon-fed. In the model of group dream work that I have found works best, listeners truly are receivers, facilitators, mirrors. Giving advice, even the best advice, is contrary to supporting a person's process, because the recognition needs to come from the dreamer. Also, good advice is often resented later. If a dreamer asks for advice, that is entirely different, but please be careful, even then. We really do not know what is best for another human being. Let's be honest and admit we barely know the right path for ourselves most of the time.

3. Generalizing the Dreamer's Experience

Another difficult issue in group dream circles concerns the "we" statements that members make in response to a dream that touches the whole group. Every group has had a powerful experience with a member sharing a dream. Personal material is one's most vulnerable offering; it stirs up the realm of associations that take us to our uncensored fantasies and memories, and what could be more naked and revealing? With the group's help, the dreamer has come to some awareness about the dream, as well as releasing and sharing emotional material with a supportive circle of listeners. Then some participant makes this mistake:

"A lot of us women have experienced abuse and discrimination, and we need to find our voices and make our reality known to all of those around us."

One word to avoid in responding to a dream is "we." Rather, a listener might respond to a dream by saying something like, "Your dream really touched me, because my daughter .... but, after she died, I felt ....," but responses like, "We all need to be more independent" are a denial of both the dreamer's and the listener's individuality and can even sound judgmental. It is fairly natural, even socially automatic for one to react with, "We all need to find our voice" or "Men like us are always having problems with football types," but generalizations cut short the process of the dreamer, as well as the group. In contrast, a listener might say something like, "Your dream moved me, because I also have a handicapped child, and at times I have felt ... ." Paradoxically, a comment that is entirely personal can open and broaden the dreamer's work, increase the listener's awareness and deepen the group's level of trust.

This is one time when the intuitive personality can get in the way. Intuition looks down the road, sees the big picture and can create a syndrome out of one or two sketches – but not always with accuracy. Intuitive people are often drawn to dream work, so this is a persistent problem in dream circles. Sit on your intuitions, please. Ask yourself what *you* are feeling right now, stay with *your* emotions and don't jump for the broad generalizations that intuition drives.

4. Evaluating the Dream

As stated earlier, it is a no-no to declare any dream good, bad, important, unimportant, etc. Dreams are like children; it is helpful to refrain from comparisons. One person in dream circle does not have "incredible" dreams while another has only "plain" dreams. This is a common and damaging mistake to make. Each dream, no matter what the content, is precious information, a treasure from the sea that has washed up on our shore. One would be completely remiss if each discovery were not given equal importance and attention.

5. Care-Taking

Care-taking is another seemingly well-intentioned attitude that can prevent truth from emerging and being sorted out. Saying what you think another person needs or wants to hear, rather than what you are really feeling, is a form of seeking control. Taking care of me often means that you feel you can control what I do or feel. Let's say that a group has run out of time, and the members ask the dreamer, still telling her dream, if she is finished. She says, "Yes," since that is what she is supposed to say and because it's convenient for the group. But what if she isn't finished at all and needs more time? Here the dreamer is taking care of the group. Or perhaps, when the group hears a sad story about a young adult son who is not getting his life together, they feel eager to tell about their sons and nephews who did get *their* lives together, thus implying that this son will, too. However, trying to take care of the dreamer (and perhaps other listeners who may be uncomfortable) can easily hinder the opportunity for feelings and images truly to resonate for the dreamer. Try to identify all the ways your group has been care-taking in the past, and see if you can imagine different ways to respond.

6. Failing to Tell the Truth

Speaking only what is true for you can be difficult, but emancipation of the spirit requires knowing who you are and having the courage to express your reality, even though speaking the truth can have serious consequences.

The truth is usually difficult to recognize. Many people who've come to my office have said, "If I could know who I am, I would know what to do," or "If I knew how I felt, I would feel it." Others know how they feel, but either they do not think that speaking for themselves is worth the effort, or they fear that the ensuing conflict would be too great. But truth telling is essential for relationship. There are things that need to be spoken honestly, and holding them back leads to trouble. Courageous exploration of your dreams may help you discover your truth, and trust within a dream circle can help you understand and express it more clearly.

Let's say that someone in the group has made a comment that hurt your feelings. You have told yourself that person didn't really mean to hurt you, or that it doesn't matter, that you should just get over it. Or you decide your feelings are probably unimportant, and if you share them, no one will like you anymore. All of these common thoughts and fears discredit our courage and sense of authenticity.

Know that if you speak your truth with respect for the other person, you will have begun a level of intimacy that few are able to achieve. It is important for your group to practice ways to say difficult things candidly and without causing more conflict and hurt.

To speak only for yourself, you can begin difficult statements with phrases like the following:

"I don't think you meant to hurt my feelings, but … "

"I wish this didn't bother me, but … "

"I know this may be entirely my problem, but … "

"I want to be closer to this group so I need to talk about … ."

For example, a group member might say something like this:

"I am afraid to say this because I don't want to upset the apple cart, but I must admit my feelings were hurt last time because S. told me to be more assertive. That may be true, but I still felt bossed around. I know I had a bossy mother, so this is also partly my issue, but I need to say this so I won't carry resentment later."

While telling the truth is important, it is just as important for the member being confronted with that truth not to put up a defensive barrier. If the leader or another member is the object of another's anger, envy, resentment, or fear, let the experience into the circle without defense. It does not help to respond with: "But I was only ..." or, "I'm not bossy at all, I'm the only one in this group who gets anything done ...," etc. Some examples for meeting painful confrontations openly are:

1. "Tell me all about it." (open curiosity); and
2. "I can see what you mean," or "I would feel the same way in your situation." (empathy).

Telling the truth, paired with curious, empathic responses will help to create a dream group that can be life-changing for its participants.

Here's one classic way a conflict might easily go unnoticed: one member, often the "powerful" one, says or does something she does not realize hurts another, more insecure member's feelings, and sparks an angry reaction. Or perhaps, during the summer, two or three members will miss the next meeting, so the day to meet is rescheduled, and in this hypothetical case, one member is left out of the new meeting, schedules being so complicated it was impossible to accommodate all members. Typically the member left out will be new or lacking in power within the group dynamics, and will keep silent, though quietly seething about the perceived slight. Inevitably, something similar will happen again, and that quiet member will be the one not to share during a meeting, because, for example, the group ran out of time. This will inflame an old wound that adds emphasis to a life-long complex of being invisible in the family, being chosen last for a sports team, etc. Eventually, the mutely suffering member will leave; the group has re-created old family dynamics that are simply too painful to endure. Had he been able to speak the truth when hurt feelings first arose, the outcome could be entirely different for both the group and that unhappy member. The member could simply have said:

"I know the decision to schedule group at a time when everyone but me could come may not have been a personal snub, but that's how it seemed, and I felt terribly hurt anyway." That could open a useful dialogue. A facilitator might answer:

"Wow, your reaction seems perfectly understandable – would you like to explore this further?"

The willingness to claim part of the problem as one's own issue (personal responsibility), and the empathic response of a member of the group with whom one is angry can open the door to a very different outcome. Being kind is not care-taking, and the truth really is liberating.

Dream circles in which each member learns to listen attentively and non-judgmentally, to focus on his or her own reality and process, and to speak only the truth will create a sacred place for personal growth and transformation. Learn to avoid the common pitfalls that block or hinder the process, and your dream circle will be well rewarded.

To Tell the Truth Exercise

In group, practice by taking turns telling your truth. Begin your sentences with, "What is true for me is … "

This is not the time to dig up old hurts and resentments; it is an opportunity to speak openly and freely about what is true for you. Make statements that are only about you. Rather than saying,

"What is true for me is that Julia is acting like a coward with her daughter." one could say instead, "What is true for me is that I am uncomfortable when Julia talks about her daughter, because sometimes I think I was a bad mother," or, "What is true for me is that I fear change." After the group has taken several rounds of the exercise, talk about how this exercise felt for you. What did you learn or observe from doing this together? How close and trusting is your group now?

Nightmares are Gifts

Let's talk about nightmares. What are they, why do we have them and what do they mean? I have been consulted over the years simply because people want their nightmares to stop. In fact, nightmares were the reason I was asked to lead a dream group at the Dallas County jail. Incarcerated women and men often woke up screaming or crying and disrupted the "tank." I was called in because nightmares were such a problem.

Actually, they are a problem. But nightmares are also gifts, some of the best gifts we ever receive, because they are the "dream-maker's" creation, they are free and they "care." In recent years, I've come to describe nightmares as messages from the divine; they are some of the most important dreams we have. An important point Jung has made is that *everything* in one's dream is something one needs.[1] What do I mean by that?

Nightmares appear to care about us because they are striving to get our attention: they are red flags, flashing lights, warnings. Something is amiss, needs immediate consideration, and may require significant change as well. As humans, we don't always adapt to change very well, so we frequently need to be persuaded to make headway. Do you actually think you would have studied for a test if you hadn't expected grades at the end of the semester and, eventually, that degree? Nightmares are something like a report card or a state of the union address.

---

1 Jung, *Children's Dreams: Notes from the Seminar Given in 1936-1940*, p. 19

The dream-maker uses images in our nightly dramas that are hyperbolic, overstated. Exaggeration helps us to get the point. Perhaps you have noticed how easy it is to dismiss dreams by thinking, "This is really weird; I only dreamed this because I am worried." Or simply, "Dreams are stupid." These and other excuses are *all* natural ways to discount and ignore dream material, especially when it is disturbing. But ignoring nightmares, just wishing them to disappear is precisely what the dreamer must not do.

Let's look at some specific examples:

> *I dreamed I saw my five-year-old daughter kidnapped by evil men and tied to a post. She was bound and gagged with duct tape, and the men restrained me as well. They forced me to witness her slow, painful rape. I woke terrified.*

The dreamer was deeply haunted by this dream. It is not abnormal for a father to fear his daughter could be the victim of a crime, but in this case, since his daughter was in fact nearly twenty, that clearly was not the point of the dream. In reality, the young girl in his dream who wore his daughter's face was an aspect of the dreamer himself, and so were the "bad guys." Seen from this perspective, it was possible to speculate about what the dream was saying to him. Certainly the "young, vulnerable, not fully mature self" symbolized by the daughter was in psychological and spiritual danger; the dreamer was torturing himself about something in his waking life. As it turned out, he was having a very difficult time in his marriage. His wife had given him an ultimatum: he had to contribute more to the family financially, or she would divorce him. As a schoolteacher, his income, though steady, was limited. This was an agonizing double bind for the dreamer's inner self. He loved being a teacher, and his wife's ultimatum seemed to put his developing feminine side in real jeopardy. I do not think it a coincidence that he had been employed as a teacher for five years, the age of his daughter in the nightmare.

So how does one approach a nightmare? First, one reason our dreamer had this nightmare was that he was trying to ignore how torn he was over the situation at home. He was doing his very best to deny it, and that is exactly why the dream-maker created a scary dream: to get his attention. The dream calls for the dreamer to realize that he is in real danger; a valuable but still delicate part of him needs protection. The inner Self, the author of our dreams, knows when we are in psychological jeopardy and creates our dreams to warn us, using symbol and metaphor just as the ancients used stories to explain and teach. In this case, there wasn't a specific action for the dreamer to take in the "real" word, but a change of attitude was imperative. The dreamer knew already that giving up teaching was not a possibility, so he needed to be more aware, more conscious – to realize that as frightening as divorce might feel, it would not be fatal. It would be far more life -threatening, as he read the dream, to give up teaching to please his materialistic wife. His marriage situation was so unpleasant that marriage therapy might have been an appropriate course of action, but the couple had already tried counseling without success. Realistic appraisal of his unhappy situation was demanded; facing it honestly would allow the dreamer to discover a more enlightened perspective on his dilemma, and perhaps even enable him to be kinder to himself. He certainly needed less of the inner dialogue with which he denigrated and blamed himself, and more of the understanding of, and compassion for himself that is needed for a mature, healthy personality to thrive regardless of life's circumstances.

One of the gifts of dream work, and especially nightmares, is that we receive information about ourselves that is beyond normal awareness and that we have denied. Best of all, we can learn to appreciate the nightmare as being motivated to confront, instruct and heal – like all good teachers.

Compensation is an important concept in dream work, one that must be considered in a discussion about nightmares. Dreams usually compensate for our conscious attitudes and beliefs so they can balance our tendency to be one-sided. Nightmares compensate for the effort to deny our true feelings, and exaggerated images in dreams are a way of counteracting our skewed opinions. One way compensation commonly reveals itself in dreams is to portray our best friends and lovers in a diminished way, and our enemies in a glorified way. Clearly something needs adjustment, and it is the shock, the necessary correction, that creates a balance.

Exercise

In your dream circle, talk about and refine your process by using the techniques you've gleaned from working with dream images to explore nightmares. I hope it is obvious to all members of your dream group that this material is especially sensitive, and has to be treated respectfully and gently. Be sure to remember that nightmares provide, in exaggerated form, just what one needs to face obstacles in one's inner life, relationships and outer world. The image may be frightening simply because it is so new. Take special note to see if some of you have had similar nightmares, and be on the lookout for common themes in your dream circle.

Dancing the Dream

When the time is right and your dream group is ready to reach a new level of trust, dancing your dreams is a powerful and fulfilling experience[1]. Each person in the group needs to select: (a) a dream that has had (or is having) a profound effect on her psyche, (b) a piece of music that reflects the mood or tone of the dream, and (c) props that complement the dance movement. Scarves, rattles, hats, masks, artwork, or anything else symbolic of the images and content of the dream may be useful.

It is essential that everyone in the group take part. Without full participation, some members remain safe voyeurs, while the rest risk foolishness and vulnerability. Sharing a creative performance work with a group brings a deep experience of intimacy. Therefore, unless everyone participates, there will inevitably be an imbalance, possibly even fragmentation of the group. This is precisely why I announce far in advance of dream retreat registration that dancing your dream is a non-negotiable required activity. Dancing a dream is not a performance, and does not require experience or talent as a dancer. It is the sacred embodiment of dream material involving the entire group. You may worry that you would make a fool of yourself, and hesitate to risk embarrassment, but that is precisely the point. It is taking the risk to be a fool that carries us to

1 Chodorow, *Dance Therapy and Depth Psychology: The Moving Imagination*

the sacred dimension of personal growth, and initiates us into the lineage of the spiritual warrior.[1]

Your dance will be your unique creation, symbolic of your own spiritual and intellectual growth. For example, a poet who had discovered a new, more meaningful poetic form made lines of masking tape on the floor and, following the tape, walked his "tightrope" as he tore an old poem into pieces and then gathered the pieces and made a fire with them.

Another dreamer, a woman who discovered a surprising sense of humor in her dream work, made herself up like a mime and as "Cirque de Soleil" music played[2], she pantomimed a hysterically comical act of trying to "find her dream" while it was written on a large piece of white cardboard and pinned to her back. Others have simply expressed their dreams with movement. They have chosen flowing, graceful motions to express serenity, or punches and kicks to express anger, frustration and despair. Some have covered themselves with scarves and slowly emerged out of that symbolic chrysalis as the music built to its crescendo, while others have danced and leapt all over the room, surprising other members in the group with their energy and flexibility.

Dancing your dream is an openly creative and uniquely personal effort. Make of it what you will, as long as it symbolizes your personal, spiritual, or intellectual growth.

When each person has completed his or her dance, thanking the dancer is all that is needed. Applause is a secular response to the offering, so I discourage it, but your group will find its own rules. When everyone has finished, group members may want to process the experience. Some will be terribly moved by a dance, and it is important to allow members to talk about how they feel after the

1 It is to Edith Wallace, Jungian Analyst and art and movement therapist, who taught a psychological dance process in her tissue paper collage workshops, that I give credit for the use of dance in group work.

2 For more information, see: www.cirquedusoleil.com/CirqueDuSoleil/en/Music

experience. This is not feedback; just as dreams are not evaluated, neither is a dream dance, nor any other creative expression inspired by dream material. In one retreat, all I could do was cry each time someone danced because the work was so touching and vulnerable.

Exercise

Dance your dream. Agree that all members will participate, and set a special meeting for this activity. It is possible you will need a different location to meet, one that has plenty of room, or better flooring and acoustics than what you regularly use. This event may also take longer than you usually set aside for dream group, so it may be helpful to plan a meal together afterward, or a chance to have a "cool down" time for lots of processing. Being careful to avoid any evaluative comments ("Jane's dance was so good!"), or we statements, ("We all did so well!") encourage the members to explore their feelings and experience. What emotions were provoked in you? Longing, fear, love, hope? What surprises did you discover for yourself, or for the group? If your dream circle has evolved into an ongoing group, you might want to make this an annual event.

Difficult Moments

Difficult moments can and will occur in dream groups. They are natural, common, and in and of themselves, nothing to fear. What is most important is how they are handled in the group; that is, how dissension is processed. Research on trauma reveals that what happened is less significant than not being allowed to talk, feel and share with others about what happened.[1] An important aspect of abuse is the silence that surrounds it.

Therefore, discord is an opportunity to explore, discuss and reveal issues that otherwise might remain hidden. It is concealed conflict that is dangerous; it is a poison that can contaminate a group to such a degree that its value is destroyed.

So how does one avoid a contaminating, secretive and destructive event? Unfortunately, there is no way to guarantee that won't happen. At times there are elements that are deep and unconscious and simply defy any attempt, no matter how earnest, to lessen their destructiveness. We are human beings, and we fall into hate in much the same way that we fall in love.

When group members (often two leading members who clash fiercely) fall into hate with one another, archetypal energies have been constellated in the group process.

Imagine how fruitless it would be to ask Romeo and Juliet, or any other couple lost in love, to be reasonable. They might be too young, too poor, or obviously unsuitable in some way, but once the

---

1 See Herman, *Trauma and Recovery: The Aftermath of Violence – From Domestic Abuse to Political Terror*

pair declares their love bond, there is no stopping them. Would we want to stop them if we could?

In the same way, falling into hate is a passion that goes well beyond any normal, rational understanding. Adversaries can be so full of righteous emotion and outrageous indignation that the fighting has no end other than splitting and division.

But there is a way to avoid this unfortunate occurrence, if everyone in the group clearly understands the commitments outlined at the beginning. Now is a good time to review and amplify the essential rules for preserving a group. Since all who live and breathe are imperfect and human, we have to accept that there will be times when complications need to be brought out in the open and discussed. . Here is the key: everyone in the group must be open and willing to understand each other. Members of a successful group simply cannot fall into attacking, name-calling, cruelty, defensiveness, bullying, or threatening behavior.[1] Generally, the attitude that best represents the ideal in dream circle is the conduct found at a temple service or a meditation retreat, where the setting manifests a ritualistic atmosphere that encourages one's best essence.

Here are some rules to review:

1. Honesty, Part II

If your dream circle hits an especially rocky patch, I encourage each person to tell the truth. Even if it is difficult, be honest. Avoid polite untruths. It doesn't help to hear confusing messages like, "It doesn't bother me when you talk more than anyone else," or "I am

1 In substance abuse treatment, where confrontation has been widespread, this finding was reported: "Confrontational Interventions as defined by Holder et al. are concerned with breaking down defence mechanisms, especially denial. Confrontation often involves forceful feedback aimed at countering "resistance" to change. Holder et al. found four studies of confrontation and none supported its use. It has also been suggested that confrontation might have a negative effect by increasing resistance or lowering self-esteem (Eliany and Rush, 1992). Finney and Monahan ranked the effectiveness of confrontation near the bottom of all interventions considered (22 of 24)." (Journal of Canadian Health.)

okay with the anger you directed at me last time." People can grow when they tell – or hear – the truth. Real honesty helps us find common ground.

Here is an illustration of how indirect communication and general dishonesty on the facilitator's part can destroy a group's trust. A man was attending Tai Chi classes where breath work and imagery were used. After class, the leader would ask members to share their experiences during the meditation time. One day the man came late and slipped in as unobtrusively as possible. Then, during the sharing time, he was surprised to hear the co-teacher ask his team teacher, "Do we have rules about coming late? What is our policy about interrupting class?" It was a thinly disguised confrontation that left the student who was late feeling publicly shamed, and he never returned.

Do not criticize, attack, or direct your bad mood at others. Do not snap at someone, do not make sarcastic remarks and do not keep silent as a manipulation. It is imperative to conduct yourself in the most mature and adult manner. Any time you are angry with someone, especially during dream material exploration, you know you have hit a complex and the anger is about a part of yourself that *you* need to see more clearly. See the person who annoyed you as a mirror. Anger provides an important opportunity to recognize an aspect of oneself that has needed to come to the surface. The projection will initially land on someone else before you realize it actually belongs to you, and provides an opportunity to learn more about yourself.

Communicate your feelings to the group. Be willing to say, "I am feeling left out in this group," or, "I am feeling inferior because I can't remember my dreams," or, "I am jealous of .... because she is losing weight," or, "I am thinking of leaving the group because ....." Give voice to your thoughts and musings, because they are important group material that needs to be acknowledged and addressed. When the tribal field is a reality, holding these feelings back doesn't really work, anyway, because others will intuit them, and then dynamics can get convoluted and even toxic.

2. Keep the Group in the Group

Here is an illustration: An analyst friend was co-facilitating a traditional therapy group with a psychiatrist. The two also shared an office space with secretaries and telephones. Once the group met without the psychiatrist, so my friend was the lone facilitator. The members began talking about rumors regarding the psychiatrist's impending marriage. My friend reported this to the psychiatrist later in the week when he saw him. The psychiatrist's response was: "It's in the group." What he meant was that the discussion was a group matter and so should stay there. If my friend had asked directly, "Are you getting married?" the psychiatrist would probably have answered that question, but given the way the information was delivered, he made the perfect response. All group dynamics and material, without exception, should remain in the group.

3. Explore Group Roles

Dream groups benefit from talking about group dynamics. Talk over your group dynamics and see if you can identify the role each person plays. Some examples of roles that group members commonly play are:

The Rescuer: This member tries to make sure everyone is feeling okay, happy and satisfied and can be counted on to intervene if an attack occurs.

The Gatekeeper: A person who likes to be in charge. The gatekeeper decides who will be in the group, where the group will meet, when the group will take a vacation and so on. The gatekeeper is one of the power positions in the group. He or she often starts and ends the group. While others are talking and getting settled, the gatekeeper will signal that it is time for the group to begin.

The Challenger: A contrary who is willing to bring up opinions that don't fit the rest of the group, to be unhappy when others are not, and to disagree with the powerful members of the group.

The Groupies: These are people who are too scared or shy to show much of an opinion, and simply go along with the perceived power in the group. If the power shifts, groupies may feel distressed but will quickly re-align their loyalties to the new power hitter. Sometimes the facilitator is a groupie, abdicating power to the "alpha dog."

The Visionary: This person constantly sees new possibilities in the group: how the group could change, how dreams could be discussed differently, what the dream content is revealing, etc. These people can be a real asset, but may have to be reined in if they come to believe they possess superior insight.

The Voyeur: This member is "new" even if he has been in group longer than most of the other members. Often silent session after session and sometimes claiming not to dream, s/he is a voyeur more than a participant.

Numerous other roles can be identified: Helpless Sad Child, Twelve-Step Warrior, Clown Girl/Boy, etc.

Exercise

Have each member take turns exploring their positions and roles in the group.

Here are some questions to ask:

1. What role do you see yourself playing?
2. Have you played that role from the beginning of dream circle, or has it evolved over time?
3. Do you play this role in other situations?

4. Are you aware of any way this role connects to the one you enacted in your family of origin?

5. What are the benefits and drawbacks of playing this role?

6. Is there a different role that you would rather have?

After the discussion, when each member has had a turn to share and process what insight has come from this exercise, form dyads in which members take turns playing their *desired* roles. (Group support can help players to get fully into character and explore a new way of being.) Afterward, process what happened during the role-playing. Express candidly any frustration, sadness, exhilaration or other emotions that surfaced.

Goodbyes and Hellos

When members leave, and when new members join a dream group

Hellos

When I was a school teacher, I was continually concerned about new students arriving in the middle of the school year. They often had miserable adjustment periods, ordeals I still hear about as an analyst many years later. Before long, I realized it was necessary to focus on the class experience, which appeared to be a feeling of invasion by a new element, threatening in an almost primal sense. To compensate, I made the new student special – not enough to incur the wrath of the others, but special, nonetheless. She got to be first in line that day, her name was written on the board in big, cursive script and added to the spelling list, a game would revolve around her, and a volunteer would present a mock interview with her the next day. In this way it was communicated that it was normal to be curious about a new person, and that the "new kid" was a new and exciting addition, a welcome break in our otherwise tedious public school routine. Over time, my classes looked forward to greeting new students, and results indicated that the new students adjusted quickly and more comfortably.

New members of a dream group need to be made welcome, too. They need to be treated with respect and compassion in the early days of their dream group time. Why the need to be so polite, so mannerly? Because it prepares the ground for the most desirable therapeutic outcome. Please keep in mind that dream group participation takes a lot of courage. The trust level necessary to achieve success in the dream group process requires that people feel safe exploring their shadowy depths. Kindness encourages trust; obnoxious initiation rituals do not.

Each new person should be introduced on his or her first day with the group, and then asked to tell something about himself or herself, just as all members should introduce themselves to the new person. (It is always interesting to hear people we have known well tell their stories; it offers clues about where they are in their current process.) The energy of the group shifts quickly with a new member. The new element is like adding a different color to a palette; he or she contributes a quality not encountered before. Almost immediately, the new color of thread begins to affect the pattern of the group fabric.

There will be a great many stories the new person knows nothing about, but for the most part it will not be necessary to stop the flow and explain details, since most of the content will be picked up along the way. I prefer to begin where the new member begins; they were not in the group in the past, so it isn't necessary to take them back there. The group is a "now" experience, not one that can be easily explained. Better to concentrate on the new moments than recapitulate the old ones.

After the first session, I ask the new member for feedback such as: "How does the group feel?" and, "Do you think this group is right for you?" Naturally, anyone who is not comfortable in the group is free to leave after the first session.

Goodbyes

Goodbyes are trickier. Some are relatively easy: a person has moved away, left for graduate school, retired to Santa Fe, or relocated through a job change, for example.

In these cases, my groups have almost always given the person a goodbye dinner. Whether in a restaurant or someone's home, we gather and bless (or "roast") the member who is leaving. Usually, we have had good humor and wild and glorious times. Even the difficult leave-takings when an especially important dream group member departs, have been satisfying events – close, caring and intimate.[1]

Some of these people return. Dallas, Texas has a lot of gravity. As much as people might complain about living here for one reason or another, many eventually return, because their relationships were too important to leave after all.[2]

Others will plan to return, like those who have been away for a year of travel, a sabbatical or some other temporary leave-taking. I have always delighted in seeing these people return to group; it's almost like a family reunion. Each group, though, will have to decide for itself how they feel about members returning.

And then there are the difficult good-byes, those who leave because they are angry, dissatisfied or in conflict. I have experienced plenty of those, and shudder to think of them. I shudder because of the damage left behind in the ongoing group, painful issues such as broken trust, horror and fear. I don't think people who throw temper tantrums, whether they yell, use icy cold language, or race out of the room never to return, realize just how hair-raising the effects can be for the group. They may soon be over it and feel fine,

---

1 An important member would be someone who originally organized the group, someone who made significant changes in dream group, or simply a person around whom a lot of energy swirls.

2 I can't think of anyone who has located here for the weather, the outdoor activities, or a liberal, sophisticated Dallas Zeitgeist.

but we don't feel the same. The effects will last in the group for a long, long time.

That is simply a fact, no matter how much modern psychotherapy would like to make it different. Emotion is alchemy, powerful fire, and as such, it can burn. There is a sharp distinction between an expression of honest conflict and a fit of rage; they are quite different. The first is respectful and intends to resolve conflict, while the latter is primitive, largely unconscious and, for its intended target, often traumatic and destructive. A later chapter will focus more specifically on complexes, which are at the heart of rage. When people get thrown into such complexes and toss strong emotion around the group like a hot potato, I go into super-therapist mode. Calmly, caringly, and with real urgency and curiosity, I work to clarify the matter:

You sound angry.

Can you say what this is about?

Can you tell me more about how you are angry with (me/him/her/us)?

Oh, it sounds like ..... could have ......, instead of .... Is that correct?

Is there anything more you need to say?

Do you feel heard?

How does the rest of the group feel?

Whatever the apparent reason for the conflict, the objective reality is that intense emotion has been provoked and brought to the surface. Even if a conflict seems foolish to other members or the facilitator, real patience is required to understand the core issue that has erupted into the dream field.

Here are some of the reasons people have been angry with me:

I sat in a different chair.

I looked "a certain way" when the dreamer shared her dream. ("What kind of way?" "I don't know, a certain way.")

I asked too many questions when discussing a dream.

I failed to take care of a member who was too "shy" to take her turn.

I was too polite.

I made a joke about sexuality.

I made the wrong response to a person's comment about her mother.

I raised the fee for group by $5.

All these are reasons given for why people left group. When it happens, I do not offer resistance; I simply let the person go without debate. In earlier years, I made the mistake of arguing with the complex, and would coax or manipulate the member into staying. I suppose I was afraid the group would fall apart, or worse yet, that it meant I was a bad facilitator. Also, I felt abandoned and disturbed when people left angrily. Eventually, I saw that my complexes were as alive in the dream circle as the other members' were. Now I am grateful for such humbling situations, because they have taught me in ways I consider invaluable.

Now, in each case I leave the door swinging; you can enter, you can leave. No one is forced to be here, coerced, pressured emotionally, or manipulated. Some therapists will say, "It is my professional opinion that you should continue with this group, but if you want to go against my advice, I will ask you to sign a statement that you do not agree with that suggestion." That may be appropriate for groups that deal with people with severe pathologies, but the usual dream circle is not in this category.

Some therapists will say, "If you really want to individuate, you need to be in a process, you need to be in this group to break through the barriers you are facing. " Now and then, such comments have come from members of the group. But the leader is responsible for directing such discussions, and I don't think it is helpful to frighten or pressure anyone to be in a group if she does not want to be there.

Some will even say, "It is a grave error to leave angry and unfinished. You will repeat this pattern again and again until you stay and resolve this matter." Making predictions regarding someone else's future is the height of hubris. It can also act as a curse, much like the thirteenth fairy who declared, "You will die on your sixteenth birthday!" because she was jealous that she wasn't included in the party to bless the new child.[1] The feelings we have about the person who is leaving will reveal useful information to us. What have we projected onto that person? Do we feel abandoned, rejected, or discounted? When in the past have we had feelings like this? Is this leave-taking provoking memories that are unsettled, unfinished? All these are subjects that may arise in the dream circles' discussions about people who are terminating.

If the dreamer wants to leave, that is that. Your final act of unselfish support must be to honor the dreamer's sense of what is safe, what is needed therapeutically – to allow him to go.

Leaderless groups have to be careful about this dynamic. Just imagine the pressure a group could apply if all members ganged up on the one trying to leave. Let her go. You may be confident that the right members will surface in the right order at the right time.

One of the rules my groups have developed over time is that one needs to give some notice of leaving so that members will have a session or two to take it in. The more notice people have given, the easier and ultimately more resolved the good-byes have been. Certainly, when a person has a logistical reason for leaving – a new job for example – it is considerate and helpful to let the group know as soon as possible. That way the group can process the departure, and it is less likely they will feel rejected and abandoned. Even if the person leaves simply because the group, for whatever reason, is not working for him, giving notice offers the group time to process the news to understand and accept it. The single fairest, healthiest

1 Gollanz, "Brier Rose," *Grimms' Tales for Young and Old*

aspect of leave-taking is simply to tell the truth and give the group some time to get used to the idea.

Here are some possibilities for a leave-taking ceremony, whatever the reason:

Arrange a meal outside of group time.

Take up a collection, and give a nice (but not too expensive), meaningful gift to the departing member.

Orchestrate a "memory lane" time, and recall all of the funny, difficult, awkward, exciting, synchronistic and amazing times the group will be able to remember about that person.

Give an award to the person who is going: perhaps "The Longest Dreams Award," or "The Most Shocking News Prize," or "Most Dreams About The Same Person Trophy" and so on – that is, if the person can handle a little teasing. Obviously, "roasting" a person who is leaving is appropriate only if the goodbye has been resolved in the circle.

This is an opportunity to turn loose the group's creativity. Skits, rap poems, songs and other gifts will be appreciated and remembered for a long time by all who participate – especially by the dreamer who is departing.

Exercise

Talk about accepting a new member. What does the group feel, think, or imagine about that? What are the rules you have developed for accepting new members? Then talk about good-byes. What principles can your group develop to deal with members who are preparing to leave? How can the group handle difficult good-byes in a way that allows growth?

Dream Dolls

Dolls are fascinating to cultures all over the world. One of my favorite pictures is the engraving of the Koshari,[1] who carries his likeness in miniature form in his waist sash. He is the clown of the Hopi, and second cousin to the Heyoka of the Lakota, the sacred clown who often expresses himself in contrary language and behavior.[2]

A small likeness of oneself carries a numinous quality – awe, a spark of the divine that moves us to another dimension. It comes in part from the realm of dreams, the realm of the unconscious. Creating a dream doll is another activity your dream circle might like to join in together. It may take several sessions (or parts of them) to complete fully, or it might be the members' preference to do the project independently and then share your creations in the dream circle. Your group can decide which works best. Please don't assume that this exercise is only for women. Men have made remarkable dolls, as well as all sorts of other artistic creations. It's a pleasure to see such work, because many men feel they have never had permission to make a doll or even to hold a needle and thread.

Making dolls is ancient and universal; it is the art of capturing a psychological aspect in physical form. There are two basic approaches to this activity. One can either make a doll that is a min-

---

1 For more on Kachinas, see Neil, *Kachinas: Spirit Beings of the Hopi* and Campbell, *Historical Atlas of World Mythology, Vol. 2 The Way of the Seeded Earth*

2 See: Castleman, *Op. Cit.*, Appendix: "The Heyoka Shaman"

iature of oneself, or of a part of oneself. The former might represent in a general way the sacred dream self that each of us has within at all times. For the latter, one could choose a dream character who has made a profound impact, and honor that dream image by making its likeness. An animal, a wise figure, an unexpected dream character, these are only a few possibilities. Each person can decide whether or not to make a dream doll, and just what the dream doll will represent.

Doll making can take many forms. You might simply roll tissue paper (the kind used in gift bags), and tie a string around the middle to suggest a waist. A head can be shaped by folding the paper down at the top, or tying the neck with string (like the waist). Arms may be added by using another, smaller roll of tissue paper anchored by string or yarn. The doll could then be dressed with glued-on fabric, leaves, colored paper, glitter, feathers, etc. The lower body could be cut vertically to indicate two legs, or kept as it is to indicate a skirt.[1] Another kind of doll can be made from an apple, a bottle and some fabric or tissue paper: peel an apple, carve a face out of it, and then make a hole in the bottom of the apple so that it can sit on the neck of a bottle shaped like an old Coke bottle (or something similar). Let the apple dry for a couple of weeks, until the face of the doll is wrinkled and rough. Then you are ready to drape the bottle in fabric to create the doll's wardrobe.

Or you might stuff a sock with rags, and secure it at the bottom using a needle and thread. At the sock's toe, tie off the "neck" from the "head" with a tight ring of yarn to form an armless, legless doll. You can then use buttons, yarn, sequins, fringe, or anything you like to fashion the face, hair and clothing.

A satisfying doll can easily be made from clay, which can be fired and glazed, or simply left in its natural state. (Some stores carry a "no fire" clay now as well.) Begin by fashioning the body;

1 Hot glue is an inexpensive but invaluable tool in this and other art projects, allowing one to attach firmly heavy objects like buttons and stones to almost any surface.

since clay is heavy, a doll about the size of your hand will be more easily managed and less likely to break than a much larger figure. After the clay has cured, it can be carved and shaped further with a knife. Curing is a slow drying process – putting your pieces under a loose covering of plastic for a few days should provide you with the desired result: a dark, firm clay that is still soft enough to shape with tools. The figure can take on as much detail as the dreamer wishes, since the face and other features can be carved into the clay. When the doll is finished, the clay needs to dry thoroughly. Then it can be fired and glazed. Glazing can add features and clothing, or you can simply use glaze to achieve a finished look. After firing, some have added their own hair and items that have personal meaning, like certain beads, gems, or amulets, and clothes can be made and used to finish your dream doll. Another way to use clay is to make the head as a separate part, adding clothes and body later. One can make a larger doll this way.

Supplies for making a more traditional doll can be found at a good craft store. One can find heads, bodies and all of the essential supplies to make a doll from scratch. A manufactured doll can be modified for this exercise as well. For those comfortable with a sewing machine, the possibilities are even greater. One can cut a pattern, sew two sides together inside out, and reverse and stuff it. A small doll can be made rather easily this way using hand stitching.

Other dolls can be made using *papier maché* to form only the head, or both body and head. (Instructions for *papier maché* are in a later chapter on making masks, and can also be found on *papier maché* packaging, or on the Internet.) The final product can be painted and varnished to provide a finished look. Other dolls can be created entirely out of natural elements: sticks, dried grasses, stones and twigs can all be assembled with hot glue to form a body, while the head may be a large seed pod, a piece of bark, or a thick leaf. One can even make a doll by piling river stones on top of each other; beginning with the largest at the bottom, it's not hard to form a complete figure with two or three rocks. Features and hair can be added with acrylic paint, or by gluing other materials in the proper places. You and your group may well discover other variations, or entirely different ways to fabricate your dream doll expressions. I urge you to explore and create together freely to access all of the playful energy available in the dream circle.

The final step in the process is to share, discuss and process the dream dolls you've made. Exhibit all of them, so that the group can examine everyone's creations. Dreamers always benefit from talking about what the doll means, how it felt to build the doll, if it has brought any new material to consciousness, and so forth. By now, your dream circle is most likely a trusting vessel in which members can feel free to explore their psyches together.

Finally, I recommend that you keep your dream doll in a special place, to signify the energy you have for exploring your dreams. Many dreamers have a home altar where the dream doll would find a fitting place. Your group might decide to bring its dolls each time you meet as an outward symbol of what you, as a group, honor among yourselves. The dolls might actually be on display together for a time at the home or office where the group meets. You may not want your doll very far from you, since it now carries the attribute of *participation mystique* – the mystical and magical quality of objects.[1]

Exercise

Determine how you will proceed with dream doll making: make a plan, a schedule and a commitment. Do not yield to any resistance that might want to discount this activity as worthless or childish. Think of it as dream-play, creative and ancient. See if you

1 For more information, see the works of anthropologist Lucien Lévy-Bruhl, who wrote six volumes on the psychology of indigenous peoples.

are now more open and willing to take risks than before. Fall into the fear so you can move through and beyond it. After the doll making is complete, be sure to share and process the experience together. If you did this work independently, show your results in a special dream group session.

Part Four

Perspective

photo: Nicholas French

Recurring Dreams

Just as nightmares materialize to get our attention, so it is with recurring dreams, though in a different way. Think of a mystery novel: clues are dropped all along the way so that by the last page, it all makes perfect sense and we know who the culprit is. Within the recurring dream is a clue, one that we are fed again and again, until we understand enough that we no longer need them. Nightmares, however, are more like horror flicks – shocking, sensational and absurdly overdone – which, like it or not, is what's needed.

As a general rule, recurring dreams fall into three major categories. Naturally, dreams are so complex and multi-faceted that stating categories will also underscore various exceptions. This grouping is meant as only a beginning point; add to the list over time if you wish. Each of the next three chapters will deal with a different type of recurring dream.

A. The Trauma Dream

The first category is described as the trauma dream, and involves a frightful situation that is replayed over and over in the dream state. These dreams are virtually carbon copies of the actual incident. There is no symbolic meaning, and no interesting figures emerge; the same event is simply replayed like a movie. These are rather rare. You are not having a trauma dream unless it is a repetition of an actual event you have suffered.[1] Holocaust victims have reported such haunting dreams, as have people who have been viciously mugged, or have endured a tragic automobile collision. By definition, trauma dreams simply reiterate extremely challenging experiences. How is this helpful to the soul, and where is the kindly dream teacher in this deeply disturbing dream? One answer might be found in behavioral psychology.

One of the ways trauma is reduced involves a desensitization process.[2] For example, a therapist will help an agoraphobic leave her house little by little. At first, the therapist will simply open the front door and have the patient look outside. Then she will have the client take a step out onto the front porch; next, walk down the sidewalk, and so on, until the person can actually go out in public. Deep breathing, meditations, relaxation exercises, rewards and many other methods are used to help the individual achieve emotional freedom from this crippling affliction. In this way, desensitization is a process of gradually exposing people to what they fear. Apparently, something similar has happened to all of us who view so much violence on film and TV: what used to shock now seems almost ordinary, or even absurd.

---

1 Jung, *The Structure and the Dynamics of the Psyche, Collected Works*, Vol. 8 par. 499

2 According to *The Encyclopedia of Mental Disorders*: "After learning relaxation skills, the client and therapist create an 'anxiety hierarchy.' The hierarchy is a catalogue of anxiety-provoking situations or stimuli arranged in order from least to most distressing. For a person who is frightened by snakes, the anxiety hierarchy might start with seeing a picture of a snake, eventually move to viewing a caged snake from a distance, and culminate in actually handling a snake. With the therapist's support and assistance, the client proceeds through the anxiety hierarchy, responding to the presentation of each fearful image or act by producing the state of relaxation. The person undergoing treatment stays with each step until a relaxed state is reliably produced when faced with each item. As tolerance develops for each identified item in the series, the client moves on to the next. In facing more menacing situations progressively, and developing a consistent pairing of relaxation with the feared object, relaxation rather than anxiety becomes associated with the source of their anxiety. Thus, a gradual desensitization occurs, with relaxation replacing alarm."

The trauma dream is just like a therapist trying to reduce the emotional baggage linked to an event, so that we can return to normal functioning. Each time we remember a terrible event, a little bit of the emotion is lifted or floats away. Eventually, one can again drive down the street where the wreck occurred, or go back to the house where a loved one died. In the dream state, the recurring trauma dream seeks this same equilibrium.

Additionally, if one continues to have recurring trauma dreams, it indicates that the emotional experience is not being adequately processed while awake. The fastest way to end these dreams is to start talking, writing and thinking about what happened to you. I can hear some of you say, "I already have discussed this with a therapist." Good! But while the dreams continue, more is needed. Even if we have dealt with – or thought we have dealt with – the material for years, there is more work to do to seek the optimal transformation. Then the dreams will stop.

EXERCISE FOR MEMBERS OF DREAM GROUP WHO HAVE TRAUMATIC DREAMS OR MEMORIES.

1. Date and record the dreams thoroughly; omit no details.
2. Write a narrative about the trauma to which the dream refers.
3. From the narrative, devise a short screenplay to depict the event. A screenplay is a distillation of your narrative in which all you have are plot, characters, setting and dialogue. This reduces the trauma much like a sauce reduction; the elements become more concentrated. Your screenplay will help to bring the vague, frightening emotional content into sharp focus.
4. With the assistance of the members of dream group, enact the play (taping it as you go). As director, you determine the action, the emotion of the actors and the camera shots.
5. View the tape.

Take adequate time to speak with the group to explore how you felt doing the exercise, and what information or insights you have gleaned from it.

B. The Long-term Recurring Dream

The second type of recurring dream, which I call the long-term recurring dream, is slightly different. It is somewhat like a trauma dream, but it isn't about any specific event the dreamer can identify. Some recurring dreams have been presenting themselves for years, or even for one's whole life.

These dreams are deep, and finding the key to unlock their mystery takes time and patience. However, it is quite possible, even probable that these dreams will resolve through conscious intent. (A recurring dream can also be a childhood dream, or a dream within a series, but those will be discussed in later chapters.)

Here is an example:

> *I dream that I am looking for my shoes. I search and search. I never can find them, and I am so distraught I awaken.*

The dreamer had this dream about once a week for several years. She was plagued by it, and found it frustrating and exasperating. She desperately wanted clarity and closure.

Over time, it became clear that one of her primary issues was about not taking action. Whether within her marriage, her relationship with her step-daughter, or her lagging professional life, she was frozen and helpless to do anything to improve the situation. With a dream group's emotional support, the dreamer started to take care of herself. She eventually changed her profession, took steps in her marriage to improve several issues, and her relationship with her step-daughter became less problematic. Then she had the final shoe dream of that recurring series:

I am at church. I see a woman there who I know is a pastor, and she is wearing shoes with pearls on them. She gives me a similar pair of shoes, and we walk out together.

Now the dream is finished, and the dreamer can move on to the next set of subjects her night-time teacher will present.

Recurring dreams can remain virtually unchanged for years, creating an enigma that the waking self cannot solve, like a riddle or Zen *koan*.[1] But then some circumstances may change, or we may see our complexes in a new light, and the dream disappears or evolves into a resolution of the kind we see in the "Lost Shoe" dream. Also, images can recur over time to give evidence of an evolution that mirrors changes the dreamer is making within him/herself.

Exercise for Long-term Recurring Dream

Focus on the waking context: recurring dreams are more easily resolved when the dreamer finally notices something in her outer life that has been ignored. Just as a telephone will ring until we answer it, or if ignored long enough, it will stop ringing, an ignored dream will go away, too. It is important for the dreamer to take inventory of her life. Some dreams that recur over a long period of time, perhaps even one's whole life, reflect issues that are so far-reaching as to imply over-arching questions few dreamers take the time to address.

Write the following questions on a lap-top or journal and answer them in detail: In general, how is my life going? How contented and fulfilled, or depressed or anxious do I feel most of the time? What are my goals for the next year? For the next five years? What is my biggest challenge, and what solutions have I found for solving it? How are my relationships? How is my professional life? How is

1 See: Isshu & Sasaki, *The Zen Koan*, and Mumonkan, *The Gateless Barrier*

my health? Where is my spiritual life taking me? What childhood wounds still affect my behavior? Add to these any questions of your own that occur to you.

Next, with your recurring dream in mind, use all of the steps that were presented in the first few chapters to understand dreams. Go over all of the associations to each dream image, outline the dream's plot, character, acts and scenes, and give the dream a title, and so on. (Be sure to associate to dream images, rather than interpret them.)

Using your dominant hand, write in your journal the question, "What does this recurring dream mean, and why do I keep having it?" Then answer your question with your non-dominant hand. This may seem impossible, silly, or merely awkward, but I urge you to give it a try. Simply sit quietly and patiently with the pen in your non-dominant hand and wait for words to come. Then, ever so slowly and attentively, let your hand write the first words you hear, and let the sentences develop with no preconceived notions. This is not automatic handwriting, but a method for writing in your journal that accesses a part of self that knows more than we do and is waiting to speak if we will only listen.[1]

Continue to write until you have a surprise, an answer or clue that you weren't expecting. This is when you know you have uncovered a treasure. Jewels of psyche are as valuable as any precious gem or gold coin.

C. Collective Recurring Dreams

The third type of recurring dream is quite mystifying. These are dreams that many of us have from time to time, or even frequently, often with striking similarities.

Some examples:

1 Capacchione, *The Power of Your Other Hand: A Course in Channeling the Inner Wisdom of the Right Brain.*

I go to my final at college only to realize I have somehow forgotten to attend class the whole semester.

I notice, much to my dismay, that I am losing my teeth. They are crumbling and falling out.

A group of very sinister men is trying to break into my house.

I discover I am in a public place and have forgotten to dress. I am entirely naked, and feel terribly embarrassed.

I am flying.

I enter my house and, to my surprise, discover I have extra rooms I didn't know about.

These are collective dreams, at least to some extent. That does not mean they lack significant personal guidance for the dreamer, but they are so similar, specific and ubiquitous that they must also be seen as information for all of us, not just the individual. In some ways they are like fairy tales, which Marie-Louise von Franz termed "collective dreams."[1] In short, she theorized that fairy tales, like myths, represent the crystallized, core psychological imprint of a culture. After the details that prove to be unimportant fade away, what is left is a story that represents a truth about a group of people. In Grimms' Fairy Tales, one sees many terrible witches and evil stepmothers.[2] One might surmise that feminine power and strength in Germany circa 1500 was manifesting in a destructive manner, while the ever-present male hero counterbalanced the female antagonist. Similarly, in dreams that are repeated in modern culture, we see broad issues being actively and energetically "talked about" by the dream-maker.

Let's examine a collective dream:

I dream that I am back in college and it is time for finals. I wander around quite a while and finally find my classroom, only to realize at

1 See: von Franz, *The Interpretation of Fairy Tales, The Feminine in Fairy Tales,* and *Shadow and Evil in Fairy Tales.*

2 Gollanz, *Op. Cit.*

the last possible moment that I have forgotten to attend any classes this semester. I awaken, horrified.

Many people dream of missed classes or forgotten exams, so this dream offers a chance to see it as being for all of us; it is a nightmare with a message that, if deciphered, could help more than just those who dream it. What is clear is that the dreamer is feeling tremendous pressure and anxiety. The dream raises a question: "How do I feel that I can't meet my responsibilities, that I am totally unprepared or trapped into failing?" Typically, the dreamer will not have an immediate answer, but if he thinks about it a while, something will come to mind that he didn't realize was bothering him so much.

One reason this dream is so common is that in our post-modern world, feeling pressure and even hysteria is a condition many face. Most of us are trying to find a way to pay bills, exercise, meditate, write in a journal, carpool, clean the house, service the car, fix meals, find time to sleep, commute, read and still go to dinner with friends. We impose nearly impossible demands on ourselves, and the current culture insists that we have to do all of these things perfectly or be seen as failures.

In the case of the "I Missed My Exam!" dream, more is at work than just reminding us that we are in a pressure-cooker culture that pushes many to the breaking point. Remember, one must be scientifically curious about *all* images in dreams, and ask, for instance, "Why is the dream setting always a college campus?" We don't dream frequently that we drive to a restaurant only to find it closed, or go to the library and find it burned down, or discover we have forgotten to pay all of our bills, etc. (the possibilities are endless). Why then is this specific image so prevalent in adult dreams? I have speculated that college, especially the first year, is such a horrifyingly tense place because both freedom and the expectation of excellence are sandwiched together, so that students, are forced to mediate this chaos.

Additionally, the engine that drives our educational system is one that employs fear, punishment, shame and blame. From her earliest school moments, the child realizes she has to "behave," which is one of her first experiences of compulsory societal conformity. Here mother's sweet voice and father's warm lap are absent, replaced by a stranger who may yell, threaten, punish or wield power in other destructive ways. Even in those cases in which one is lucky enough to have the kindest teachers, rules abide and a form of oppression remains despite those teachers' best intentions.

The child quickly has to determine the norm: is it all right to talk without raising a hand, and is it okay to sharpen a pencil without permission? Many rules have to be learned correctly and promptly, or the child is punished by ridicule, by the humiliation of being reprimanded in front of the class by the teacher, by being kept in during recess, by knowing the teacher is calling a parent, by harassment from the other children and worse. Pop quizzes, test grades, report cards and state exams all begin early and produce grave anxiety in children.

Children sense the repressed panic of both teachers and parents, and learn that high performance will ensure affection and regard from the authorities, finding as well that failure often feels like love is being withheld. For a small person, this is life or death. This pattern, one that continues throughout the educational system, is brutal and abusive. So the dream portrays it over and over in uncounted individuals' nighttime dramas – not just an "anxiety dream" (whatever that means), but a societal mistake revealed in the collective dream.

Trauma and terror mark the beginning of education, and continue throughout schooling, reaching a crescendo in college. There the stakes are life-changing: perform or flunk. Flunking is an emotional, financial, social, even professional failure that can wound a person for the rest of his life. Education is harrowing for most people, even the smarter ones. In the freshman year of college a person usually faces his greatest freedom and his greatest pressure. The choices are daunting. Do I study, or take drugs? Do I write a paper, or have sex? Do I read my assignments, or stay out late partying? Let us not forget, this is also when early onset schizophrenia begins to appear. Many young people are deeply traumatized by college, even when they do not consciously know it.

The effect becomes clearer when we follow the normal process of working with dreams. The only difference in the amplification of the educational context above is the use of the culture as the dreamer rather than an individual. Now we can begin to see how this dream might come to us as it does. Yet a collective dream will also have personal meaning that is being manifested exclusively for the individual dreamer; as usual, this must be found by associating to all images in the dream, and scrutinizing its waking context. A dream like this can indicate a person is worried about an upcoming performance or task, it can be a warning that more care needs to be taken in preparation, or it can be a confrontation about the inner school authority in one's psyche and how one is captured by that complex. But remember, it can also be something else entirely. Any answers will be found in one's dream explorations.

Another common collective dream is the ubiquitous:

I notice, much to my dismay that my teeth are crumbling and falling out.

Title: Loosing Teeth

Character: The Dreamer

Plot: I notice that my teeth are loose. Then they begin falling out.

Feelings: Shock. Horror. Fear. Embarrassment. Anxiety. A "How could this be happening to me?" feeling. Confusion.

Personal Outer Life Events: (The dreamer would have to fill this in herself, of course.) Am I concerned about my age? Am I feeling tongue-tied about an issue in a relationship? Am I concerned about change coming? Do I find others bore me, or that lately my job bores me? Am I neglecting some aspect of caring for myself? All patterns of thought, feeling, change or energy have to be tracked. Perhaps some (or none) of these pertain to your waking context, but all of these feelings ideally should be inventoried to discover to which feelings the dream refers.

This dream is also quite popular in "dream dictionaries," and you will read, among other notions, that this dream means:

1. The dreamer is conflicted about aging and has an unhealthy desire to be young.
2. A change of consciousness is coming.
3. The dreamer is using faulty logic about something.
4. The dreamer has been gossiping too much.
5. The dreamer is angry.
6. The dreamer is facing a major milestone.
7. The dreamer is experiencing loss of childhood innocence.
8. The dreamer fears loosing sexual attractiveness.
9. The dreamer fears that life is out of control.
10. The dreamer fears becoming a victim.
11. The dreamer needs to be heard, to express himself.

There are others; see the Internet for a long, varied list.

For some reason, this dream is a favorite in the dream-as-a-riddle-for-which-an easy-answer-can-be-found school. Such "answers" are all over the map. As a general rule, this dream is probably *not* about any of the issues listed above. On occasion, one of those formula answers may fit for you, but they are so general that very likely most people are dealing with one or two on the above list almost all of the time, just as the day's horoscope seems to fit anyone. Again, I must emphasize that dreams have to be treated as unique and individual material; otherwise we reduce them to the banality of everyday common thought and bias.

After you have considered your waking process, it is time to turn to the collective outer events this dream, with its encoded symbolism, is trying to reveal. Here is where symbolism dictionaries can be valuable. We do not look up the images in our dreams to learn what they mean, but to research an image to learn what it has meant to people in various locations over the span of history. This is referred to as amplification, which is quite different from the process of making personal associations.

Amplifications for teeth

Teeth help us chew our food, thus beginning the first process of digestion, ultimately transforming the food into elements we can physically assimilate. We are not born with teeth, they are acquired over our lifetime in two phases: baby teeth, which erupt about six months after birth and later fall out, to be replaced by permanent teeth beginning around age six. Teeth, unlike muscles, skin, internal organs and soft tissue have a structure that can survive long after death. Skeleton and teeth are some of the last elements of the body to remain over time.

Our permanent teeth normally stay with us through adulthood, though they can be lost to decay, injury or illness. Until recently, most adults' teeth didn't last until the end of their lives; dentures have been necessary for many in old age. Teeth can also be a cosmetic enhancement indicating youth, beauty and good health, and for a time, Europeans envied Americans for their straight white teeth. Dentists know that losing teeth is a sign of poor hygiene, poor health, or poor nutrition. Women often lose calcium during pregnancy, which can result in their dental health being compromised. Perhaps it has always been true, but now, especially, teeth are a status symbol. Success in society, film, politics or sales would not be likely with missing teeth. Over the years I have heard clients tell of experiencing abject horror and fear over losing a front tooth on vacation, or in some other circumstance. All but one retreated into absolute solitude until a dentist could rectify the situation.

In the current era, many consider straight, white teeth a real necessity. It can amount to a modern obsession. Though painful, expensive and sometimes temporary, teeth-whitening procedures make up a huge industry driven by collective vanity. In short, good teeth are sexually and socially valuable.

Bared teeth are a sign of anger and aggression in the animal kingdom, and humans display this primitive expression as well. Imagine how your mouth looks when you have been cut off on the expressway and are making guttural noises (and perhaps animated gestures) in response. Teeth would seem to be associated with power, since those with strong teeth can eat more foods, and thus have the greatest chance of survival. Teeth are weapons as well, since biting is a way to hurt, even kill another person. When we add together all of these qualities, we can see teeth as being related to a young, active, vigorous, powerful and sexual personality. Teeth, like fingernails, are a tool we have with us at all times, and can use with decisive effectiveness.

Outer Collective Events

1. As a culture, we are obsessed with appearance. We have gone mad over weight, looks, hair, facial wrinkles, chin shape, thigh circumference and more. It is impossible to turn on the television or read a magazine without being bombarded by sales jobs and product indoctrination. Be pretty! Be thin! Be perfect! Though they escaped it for years, men and children are now subject to this pressure, too. Now everyone is a target, and if you cannot do enough yourself through masochistic dieting and exercise, specialists are ready to staple, cut, reroute and reorganize your whole body from bunions to eyelids. What does this say about our culture? Are we more evolved? Are we more conscious? Are we more compassionate than in earlier times? Will future generations see our collective obsession as an aspect of progress or decline? Just having a body does not appear to be enough; the body has to be offered upon

the altar of rejuvenation to make it acceptable in society. We know that the body lies in the realm of the feminine archetype, and that surgery, knives and other objects of overt change lie in the realm of the masculine archetype. How much clearer could this mirror show us our foibles? Whether earth, body, or soul – all are victims of a violent thought process that is destructive and uncaring.

2. We are adrift in our world: modern angst, existential crises, a general malaise, these are all real and unfortunate consequences of the current era. Post-modern deconstructionism, a way of being reflective, has become popular because the object has lost its meaning. We sense that we now live in a kind of lie, a fiction that does not really satisfy, like reading the preface and skipping the book. We are lost and soulless. So many people are striving to discover direction, clarity, passion and drive. Where are they? How can I find them? Will I ever feel passionate about anything? Where are the "teeth" in my life?

3. The natural, primitive aspects of men and women, anger and aggression in particular, are being socialized out of us to such a degree that we are not allowed any real range of expression. How can a person be angry? Anger about bad driving is one thing, but what about injustice, war and illness? How we can "stick it to the man" without going to jail or comprising our values is a conundrum for our culture. Despite all the energy that was needed to evolve to the point we currently occupy, aggression is now somehow obsolete – lost in the psyche, floating around without a home and erupting inappropriately, creating a violent society that often appears out of control. War is a way the collective cultural psyche deals with aggression. We are humans, blood-thirsty meat eaters who require a certain amount of violence to regulate our temperaments. Unfortunate, but true, I am afraid. In the post-modern era, those of us who are not literally at war have to find ways to access and use our feelings effectively, positively, to institute change.

Taken all together, the teeth dream looks as though something is falling apart in the realm of effectiveness – that is, falling apart in the realm of digesting and taking in a psychological aspect, falling apart in the area of direction and clarity, falling apart in the area of expressing aggression and falling apart in the way we overhaul the body to suit the standards of a demanding, but meaningless society.

Of course you must reach your own conclusions. Such material can be worked and reworked, kneaded and allowed to rest repeatedly as it demands our continued awareness.

Exercise

As a group, choose one of the dreams listed at the beginning of this section (or one that has emerged in the dream circle) and see if you can discover the collective dream and its comment on society. Imagine how it may comment in general on the individuation process, that universal project through which we can become mature, whole beings.

This is where you enter the realm of Jungian sociology, where Jung's ideas are applied to groups, societies and cultures, as well as to individuals. We are dreamers, and likewise, our cultures dream, our nations dream – our world dreams.

The Dream Series

Actually, all dreams occur in series. Please remember, it's very important to date and record one's dreams thoroughly. Otherwise, this chapter will be useless, and the dreamer will miss an essential aspect of the process of learning from dreams. One can think about a dream series as recurrent images that evolve over time, and as they evolve, we see how our own growth is progressing – or not.

Here's another analogy: a puzzle. Think of each dream as a piece of a picture puzzle. Some of the pieces reveal a bit of the picture if we look closely enough, but as more pieces are put together, the picture becomes exponentially clearer. So it is with dreams. As we string more and more of them together, we begin to see how they are connected, and this takes place over time, since you may have dozens of dream series going on at the same time, as well as different series being woven together in a rather intricate pattern. It is beneficial to look at the dreams that both precede and follow the dream you are focusing on, because much information lies within the immediate series as well as any longer series.

Once, in a class I taught with analyst Ernie Bel,[1] we discussed this concept at length. Over time, we thought the dream series could be illustrated as a symphony. An image would contain musical notes: tree could be C major; oak tree could be C major plus E major; oak tree (C plus E major played as a chord) in a night-time setting could be C plus E in a minor key. If there is wind, a flute

1 Ernest Fay Bel, Jungian analyst, maverick and friend, who died June 30, 2001

trill could be added to the chord. In this way, a dream can be put to music. And in a series, when wind recurred, as an example, the same trill line would be added to the music. A musical code could develop over time in one's own musical dream dictionary. A dream theme would have a melody line that would be repeated each time that theme reappeared. This would eventually create a musical representation of the dream series, and illustrate melodically how dreams are connected.

Here are some examples of dream images that reappeared over time in series:

A woman dreamed of double pianos five times over the course of three years. During this time she developed her own company and achieved a professional level she never expected. The pianos have not appeared again.

A man dreamed about a particularly petite woman (about four feet tall) with dark hair, whom he had never met in his waking life. She appeared regularly in his dreams, two or three times a year over a several year period. The first few times she appeared, the dream had a sexual tenor. Later, she began bringing luggage to him. Finally, in the last dream, the dreamer opened the bag the woman carried and discovered she had brought art supplies, a gift for him.

A woman dreamed about Oz – about the ruby slippers, which became emerald slippers (Oz is the Emerald City), which then became the Emerald Tablet of Hermes, an ancient alchemical text.[1]

---

1 One translation of the Emerald Tablet, by Isaac Newton, found among his alchemical papers as reported by B. J. Dobbs:

1. Tis true without lying, certain most true.
2. That wch is below is like that wch is above that wch is above is like yt wch is below to do ye miracles of one only thing.
3. And as all things have been arose from one by ye meditation of one: so all things have their birth from this one thing by adaptation.
4. The Sun is its father, the moon its mother,
5. the wind hath carried it in its belly, the earth its nourse.
6. The father of all perfection in ye whole world is here.
7. Its force or power is entire if it be converted into earth.

One fascinating aspect of such dream series is that the dreamer is often totally unaware of the recurring images and how they are changing over time. Computers are an aid here, since one can perform a word search and find all of the dreams that may contain the word "piano," for example.

In order to identify dream series, it is necessary to list images and themes in your dreams in an index.

EXERCISE: DREAM JOURNAL INDEX

Go back to the beginning of your dream book(s). If you have years of dreams, all the better. Keep in mind that the effort we put into mining our dreams is directly related to the gold we will discover. Begin by developing a system; I encourage using a computer that is backed up and printed out regularly. A three-ring notebook with the printout punched and filed in it is invaluable.

After the date, number the dream. For each dream, list images, characters, emotions and themes.

Separate thou ye earth from ye fire, ye subtile from the gross sweetly wth great indoustry.
8. It ascends from ye earth to ye heaven again it desends to ye earth and receives ye force of things superior inferior.
9. By this means ye shall have ye glory of ye whole world thereby all obscurity shall fly from you.
10. Its force is above all force. For it vanquishes every subtile thing penetrates every solid thing.
11a. So was ye world created.
12. From this are do come admirable adaptations whereof ye means (Or process) is here in this.
13. Hence I am called Hermes Trismegist, having the three parts of ye philosophy of ye whole world.
14. That wch I have said of ye operation of ye Sun is accomplished ended.

To illustrate:

#1

June 15, 2008

I am lying in bed with P., who is also B. Obama. I know he will be president some day. He and I are only friends, but I touch his thigh affectionately with a pat. He turns to me and says, "No, (my name), don't do that." I feel rejected and hurt.

Images to Index:

P.

Bed

B. Obama

Thigh

Feelings to Index:

Affection

Rejection

Shame

Fear of Aging (P. and B. Obama are much younger than the dreamer.)

Actions to Index:

Making an affectionate advance that is rejected

Patting

Lying in Bed

Themes to Index:

Friendship being mistaken for sexual advance

Leadership potential in a young male figure

Next, put all of the items to be indexed in alphabetical order, and then put the number of the dream next to the item.

Bed-#1

Fear of Aging – #1

Lying in bed – #1

Obama – #1

Making an affectionate advance that is rejected – #1

P. – #1

Patting – #1
Rejection – #1
Shame – #1
Thigh – #1

The next time you record a dream, go back to your index and add the new items to the alphabetical list with a #2 following each entry. Naturally, you could wait to do this task every few days or weeks, depending on how frequently you dream, but keeping up with the indexing will allow you to see the benefit sooner. (You can do this now for every dream recorded, no matter how old.) Finally, one might word search "rejection" and find references in "Dreams 1, 16, 93," etc., allowing the dreamer to see the similarities and changes in the issue of rejection. If the dreams have been dated accurately, the rejection dreams can be correlated to waking life events.

A dreamer might realize, much to her surprise, that she dreamed about exactly the same "tree lighted from within" two years earlier, but had forgotten it. Or a dreamer might notice that there certainly are a lot of house dreams. Colors can be tracked, too – a red kite becomes a red bird, and that becomes a red prayer shawl. Similarly, numbers are significant; three women, four men, twins – all are images that can be indexed to help you see the big picture of your dreams. Additionally, one can quickly see how an emotion might transform over time. Just look up the item or feeling in the index, and there you will have, in chronological order, all of the dreams presenting that image, feeling, or theme. Remarkably hard work, but it brings phenomenal rewards.

EXERCISE

It could be useful and enjoyable to index your dreams together in a dream circle session. Those using computers would bring lap-tops, while others would need plenty of writing materials. The chief advantage for doing this in dream circle is that it tends to be quite motivating. (Washing the dishes with my brother was always more fun than washing them by myself.) If you do opt to do this separately, please take time to share the results in your next gathering. Was this project difficult, or a waste of time, or frustrating? Were there benefits? Insights? Process this exercise as you have the others.

The Childhood Dream

The childhood dream is a subject of much thought and research in the Jungian world. If you become interested in that area, there are articles and books referenced in the bibliography that will be helpful. A recent, invaluable publication in English is Jung's seminar entitled: *Children's Dreams.*[1]

The general description is: an early dream, usually recurring and often frightening, and one that is never forgotten.

You may have more than one childhood dream, or you may think of your childhood dream as the first one you ever remembered. It may be a dream you had twice, or it may be one that is more puzzling than disturbing. Naturally, there are endless variations of the childhood dream, because each of us is quite different from one another and our dreams are unique as well. What is most significant is that, while so much of one's life is lost and forgotten, the adult has remembered this dream throughout all his years of living.

All of these dreams can be investigated just as a recent dream would be, for the process is identical – but they are deeper and more difficult to understand. Let's recall a cardinal rule of dreams: they are prospective. That is, a dream is a prospectus, much like a weather report or a business plan. It does not predict as much as it presents a possibility of what may happen. The childhood dream depicts the salient issue one grapples with throughout life – one's

1 Jung, *Children's Dreams: Notes from the Seminar Given in 1936-1940*

karma, if you like. That issue is an over-arching matter the dreamer must try to resolve, conscious or not.

Childhood dreams can invite us to explore the possibility of reincarnation, or to puzzle over the relationship of space and time. It seems that very early in life, the dream-maker presents an issue that is carried for one's entire life. This is the childhood dream, in which the problem presented is the one that is essential to resolve during one's lifetime. It seems to me that we are all attending Life Learning School; knowing which test to study for is the principal trick. Here are some examples of childhood dreams:

I dreamed I was being eaten by a sea monster.

I dreamed witches would fly into my room at night, trying to kidnap me.

I dreamed I was flying.

I dreamed I was bouncing very high each time I ran or walked. It was very pleasant.

I dreamed my father was dead. I saw his body and knew I was supposed to put coins on his eyes. Somehow that would save him.

If you are getting nervous because you can't remember any dreams from childhood, please don't worry. Each of us has a process that is entirely our own, and not everyone has a childhood dream kept in memory over the years. Perhaps you have already resolved the early conflicts in your life, or maybe your life issues are obvious in the flow of your existence and there is no need to seek the essential challenge in the past. Whatever the reason, whether you have an early dream or not, the dreams of the present will provide plenty of opportunity for insight and growth of consciousness.

If you don't have an early dream and wish to make contact with your psyche at its youngest, see if you can recall the fantasies and fears you had as a child. Did you think there was a monster under the bed or in the closet? Were you afraid of the dark? Of water? Did you think angels came into your room at night and took you away? All of these images are similar to childhood dreams and hold treasures to discover if you challenge yourself to see them in new ways.

Exercise

Ask each group member to tell his or her childhood dream. Include all the details you can remember, what was happening in your life and family when you had these dreams, and how you felt about yourself at that time.

Then associate to all the images in your dream just as for any other dream. You may notice that you are associating (with memory) to images that were dreamed before you assume you could have developed associations. This is natural, albeit puzzling and fascinating. Often our dreams are quite a bit ahead of literal waking time, and the childhood dream is a prime example. Sometimes I envision the childhood dream as a huge arc, a life template that introduces to the developing ego the long, complete story of our lives, its essential core, path and pitfalls – the overall work project.

Include amplification of your childhood dream images (the process explored in the Collective Dream chapter). If you dreamed about three women giving you a bath, you need to research this image from every angle: mythology, religion, poetry, history and so on. One could discover a profusion of material about three women, and "bath" would need amplification as well.[1] Religion, mythology and history are filled with material that amplifies the bath: ritual bathing, baptism and rebirth are just a starting point. As you complete the amplification research, work to "connect the dots." It could be important to consider number symbolism.[2] Just as in the earlier classification exercise, in which connections are made be-

1 For an outstanding research tool, The Archive for Research in Analytical Symbolism is a website that for a small annual fee provides visual and written amplifications of nearly every subject imaginable. www.aras.org

2 Jung, "On the Significance of Number Dreams." *Dreams* pp 13-20.

tween disparate objects, we look to find the narrative that emerges when all of the amplifications are painted into the big picture of the dream. Marie-Louise von Franz referred to this as "finding the red thread"[1] in fairy tales or other archetypal material. When the group feels ready, share this work. Again, as always, the group listens and may ask questions to clarify and understand the dreamer, but no conclusions are to be drawn by the circle. The circle is the witness: fully present, fully supportive and fully detached.

Be sure to title the dream: list its characters, action, setting and mood. Settling into a calm, meditative place to collect as much of yourself as possible, list all the detail you can. After you have worked on your childhood dream, the following exercise can be helpful.

Active Imagination

In the next part of this exercise, active imagination will be introduced as an invaluable tool to help access parts of the psyche that are ordinarily hidden from the conscious self. There are dozens of ways to practice active imagination: in dialogue, art, sand tray projections and waking dreaming to name only a few. (Many are included in the exercises in this book.) In the case of the childhood dream, I will outline a dialogue technique for the dream material that can be applied to any dream, especially those that seem to have more information concealed in their characters and images than traditional associating can access.[2]

Active imagination is a tool that many people think is too hard, too dangerous or just, "Something I can't do." This is simply not

1 Personal conversation with Marie-Louise von Franz, Küsnacht, 1984

2 Those interested in a thorough explanation of active imagination with writing a dialogue can consult Progoff, *At a Journal Workshop*, or visit www.intensivejournal.org

the case. As with house painting, preparation is the key. Those readers who have knowledge of painting know that without proper sanding, stripping, scraping and repairing of the surface, painting a house is an awful mess. The most valuable time and effort lie in the preparation, not the painting. Using the analogy of house painting, prepare to allow your psyche to speak to you. First, create a quiet, sacred space where you won't be interrupted,. Have your laptop, or special notebook and favorite pen in your lap or at a table, so you're ready to write. Relax and sink into the deeper layers of your memories, your history. You may benefit from music, incense, candles, drumming, yoga, hot water relaxation, and so on. Find your center before you begin; this is the key step of preparation.

Now see yourself at age fifteen; what did you look like? Where did you live? Who were the members of your family? Next, go back to yourself at age ten and recreate that time in the same way. When you picture yourself, what do you see? Feel your way into the person you were then. Let the images float up to you, not grabbing at them or directing them in any way. Simply let them emerge, allow them to come to you. Then go back to the age you were when you first had your childhood dream. See yourself at this age, noticing what you wore. How was your hair cut? Who were your friends? What did you do when you played? Did you go to school? What was your life like? As you conjure up this young presence of yourself, ask that young person to talk with you.

Then take your pen and write:

To myself at age . . . : (fill in your childhood name and age, or if you don't know the age, identify yourself by a verbal sketch, such as, "To Buddy when we lived in Chicago in the green house," for example.)

I value who you are and what life was like for you. I am still you but covered by so many life experiences that I would like your help in remembering things about you. Would you be willing to talk to me?

Then wait quietly and listen for an answer. This is not automatic handwriting, though at times it may almost feel like that, but it is powerful and it does work if one is patient. Just listen for the first thing you hear, and write it down. Do your best not to censor or edit, just let it flow.

As the answers come, continue to write more questions. Write the questions you have now, and then put down the answers as they come from yourself in the past. Keep in mind that some neuroscientists find strong evidence that all of our memories are stored.[1] All of you is there; all you have to do is invite yourself to come forward and help you remember.

Then ask your younger self what she associates to the images, just as you would in dream group.

You can also ask your younger self to speculate about what the dream means.

Complete the dialogue part of this exercise in about 15-20 minutes. (You may finish quicker, but going on longer is not advised.) Finally, ask the group members to share their insights and frustrations, as well as the information gathered in the exercise. Naturally, not all material need be shared unless the dreamer wishes to do so. This exercise is different, and probably more advanced, than writing with your non-dominant hand, because nothing is forced. This is quite similar to the process that Jung used.[2]

Additional Exercise

Make a collage from your childhood dream.

Using magazines, handmade papers, colored tissue paper, found objects (as before: pebbles, pressed flowers, leaves, dried grasses,

1 See: Berne, *Games People Play: The Basic Handbook of Transactional Analysis*, or visit www.itaa-net.org

2 For more on this remarkable technique, see: Hannah, *Active Imagination: Encounters with the Soul as developed by C. G. Jung*, p. 146

seed pods, twine, or anything you can glue to paper), create a picture about your childhood dream. This does not have to be a literal depiction, but can be an impression of your experience, both of the dream when you had it, and the experience of processing it at your current age.

This exercise can feel like homework, or it can be much more fun; the bonding forged by devoting one dream group to creating it together is striking. Each person can bring supplies from home, and the group members can work side by side on their dream art. A big dining room table works well; just be sure to use a heavy white cardboard or some other material that will support the weight of your collage.

Share with each other – always. Process, listen and feel together. Hear each other's pain, joy, suffering, recognition, healing and insight.

Part Five

Expertise

photo: Carolyn Brislawn

Dreams that Confuse

It is time to review one of the basic and most difficult aspects of dreams: a lot of the time they don't seem to make any sense. Some dreams simply refuse to shed any light, provide clear guidance or reveal clues for our lives, no matter how much effort we put into deciphering them. They may become clearer over time, and then again, they may not. And yet, many dreams do pour out gems of fascinating and clever insight, if only we are patient and stay with the process long enough. But how to know the difference; how does one know, so to speak, when to stay in the game and when to fold your hand?

Well, the answer is that there is no certain answer. You simply have to feel your own way into this over time, and after working with your dreams for a while, you will know when to rest if the dream is not budging. It is perfectly acceptable to let a dream go if it is totally mystifying. At times, there is an advantage in letting a dream go, since it makes clear the subordination of the ego to the dream-maker. This is an experience of maturity, of adult behavior, of knowing that we don't know.

Again and again, people rush to conclude, pat dry and put on the shelf dreams and their mysteries. Recently, at an international conference on dreaming, I had just this discussion with a fellow author on the subject of dreams. "Well, I have big dreams and then just those little meaningless ones, too," she told me. When I admitted, "I am not so sure I even believe in big dreams," she looked at me quizzically and said in her clipped British accent, "Well, I can't agree with you there!" She went on to say, "You know, I have those typical anxiety dreams, and I really don't think they are difficult to understand." It was a real challenge not to launch into a lecture about dreams occurring when we need to know something, not when we are already aware that we are anxious. I did tell her how I thought a "typical anxiety dream" might hold a nugget or two of insight, and after we sparred back and forth a while, she graciously accepted my point. I acknowledged to her that some dreams certainly seem bigger than others. And perhaps they are. Almost everyone is tricked by the dream-maker on occasion into believing a dream image doesn't matter much. Even professionals who work with dreams regularly can be hoodwinked by an ego that prefers to skip over the least bit of ambiguity.

It is a fulfilling experience to remain open-minded, to enjoy the liberating experience of saying, "I don't know." There will be times when the dream group will need to give up on a dream discussion, to let the dream go until a later time. Revisiting dreams after a while can be a surprising and delightful way to work on difficult dreams, because a dream might suddenly clarify itself.

I certainly recall dreams, my own and those of my analysands, which have taken literally years to understand. Sometimes that is because there are elements in the dream that are outside your immediate knowledge, even though you dreamed it. You simply have to be patient until the day comes when you run across some information that unlocks your dream like a key in the front door, and there you have it! Could you have researched it and found the clues earlier? Perhaps, but in some cases you may not recognize that you have dreamed about a Mayan myth or an Iroquois tradition until you happen to encounter that information somewhere.

Some dreams anticipate events that will happen in our lives. Difficult as this may be to believe, it is so. Those who work with dreams extensively know it, because we have observed the almost casual way dreams comment on issues and events that have not yet occurred. In this way it is quite easy to understand how a dream would not make sense until later.

One by one, ask each dream group member to share a dream that, so far, has baffled him or her. Then, after discussing the dream using the protocol outlined in this workbook, see if the group can help the dreamer uncover some associations and thoughts that might illuminate the dream. If not, let the dream stay in the oven; it is not finished baking.

If you succeed in finding a dream that is an absolute puzzler, here is a trick that is fun, and can quite mysteriously aid in penetrating the dream's meaning.

EXERCISE: THE MYSTERY BOX

Find a box that pleases you. It can be a department store box, a shoe box, a tin box, a wooden box – whatever you have or can make that signifies a special, sacred container for mysteries. As in any activity that has to do with dreams, the more effort put forth, the greater the harvest reaped. Your dreams will usually reward you when you go to a creative and daring place in your soul.

This box will hold your mystery dreams. Make a copy of the dream that is too hard to understand just yet, and put it into an envelope; this is now a letter that you can address to your dreammaker. Then put the dream-letter into the box and close the lid. Choose a place in your home, prominent or private, to display your box. This is where your mystery lives, where your dream is gestating – alone to transform quietly, to become what it will be.

The day to open your box and see what is inside will come. Perhaps the dream will still be as opaque as before, but perhaps not.

Dreams That Clarify

There are also dreams that appear to be quite the opposite of the mystery dreams discussed earlier. These are dreams whose meaning seems – and in fact may be – obvious. One exclaims, "Oh, I know exactly what that means!" And perhaps one does.

But, as I think the readers of this guidebook have learned by now, it is also important to be careful about hasty judgments. Here is a trick your dream group can play with:

Choose a dream that is simple, obvious and clear. Then say the opposite of what you think the dream is telling you.

Here are some illustrations:

> *I see C.B., and he gives me a big hug. He touches my breasts, and it is erotic but also friendly. He tells me he used to hate me because I never did my homework, but he is glad to see me again now, and likes me better.*

The dreamer's associations to C. B.: Brilliant, creative, a musician, an excellent teacher, but very difficult, fascinating.

The dreamer's life situation: Recently divorced and excited about her new life, but avoiding any new social contacts, romantic or otherwise.

The dreamer thought this dream was obvious: "I am now encountering a new part of myself that I wasn't able to know before ("*I used to hate you but not now*"). I need to trust that my new life will be all that I want it to be, and reach out to my more fascinating musical side."

I asked her to say the opposite:

"I am not encountering an old part of myself that I was able to know before (but didn't, for some reason). I should not trust that my new life will be all that I want it to be and should not reach out to the musical side of myself."

This exercise brought up some interesting insights for the dreamer, because she was shocked to admit that both statements were true, her obvious thought about the dream and the opposite perspective. It can be enlightening to try this method with any dream, but especially the ones we think are obvious.

Exercise: Heyoka Dreaming[1]

Have the group try this exercise with dreams on which you have already worked. Go around the circle and state the meaning you gathered from the dream into opposite language, as was illustrated above. Afterward, discuss the process and your experience:

How does this feel?

Did you find new information from this process?

What seems true now?

Is this a useful method for you to try with puzzling dreams?

The Really Obvious Dreams

There is a special category of dreams that are obvious, and no amount of playing around with opposite messages will deter the dreamer from understanding the dream-maker's announcement.

These dreams are rare, maybe one or two in a lifetime. They usually indicate the need for change in the waking world, and after

1 Castleman, *Op. Cit.*, pp. 176 & 233-254

receiving the dream, its dreamer is usually clear about what needs to change.

At the risk of repeating myself, this is something that only the dreamer can be certain about; the group acts only as midwives. It is potentially very dangerous for group members to assert that anyone should take a specific action, such as divorce, stopping chemotherapy, quitting a job, moving out of town, or cutting off a relationship with a family member. It is only for the dreamer to decide about such changes. Yet these are the sorts of changes that the 'I know for Certain" dreams are getting to; major life changes that may require a push from the Self to give the ego the courage to take the risk.

By now, your dream group may be well bonded, a pretty tightly knit circle. That, of course, is the goal. You may think that at a certain point in our relationships we have achieved a bond that allows me to tell you what I think you should do in your life. After all, we know each other well now; we are friends. You know that I only have your best interests at heart and wouldn't tell you anything that wasn't true, helpful and correct. If your group has gotten to this point, *STOP!* Go back to the beginning of this book and reread the basic rules of dream work in a group setting. Without healthy boundaries, your group could disintegrate into a circle that is not about dreams, but something entirely different. It's a good time to review together this list:

I do not know what your dream means.
I do not know what your dream wants you to do.
I do not know what your dream is telling you to feel.
I do not know what your dream shows about you.
Your dream is neither a positive nor a negative dream.
The image(s) in your dream neither predict disaster nor good fortune.
However, you may determine any of these factors for yourself, and I will validate your sense of what is right or true for you.

Let's look at a couple of dreams whose meaning was clear as soon as the dreamer had awakened. These dreams required only that the dream circle be witnesses and hold the sacred space for the dreamer as she related the dream.

The dreamer was working for a man with whom she was having an affair. She worked over ten hours a day, more than five days a week and also had a husband and two young children. Her boss was the head of a large company, and was influential and successful in the community, unlike her husband, who was underemployed and passive. They all lived a smallish town, so the boss heard gossip about the husband, who, it turns out, was also having affairs. The dreamer wanted to hear none of that, so to drown out the impending disaster, she worked more, drank more and started running up to six miles a day.

Here is the dream:

> *I am at my office. I have on armor, a shield, a sword and a helmet – I look like Joan of Arc. I realize the office is being invaded by my enemies, and I have to fight my way out of the dungeon I am in. I lop off legs, arms and heads. Each time, blood spurts out in a gory, horrifying mess. I make it to the boss's office and he is not there, but I see curled up underneath his desk a large snake, maybe a foot in diameter and fifty feet long. It has no neck, but is sort of like a giant worm. I see its pale blue eyes staring at me, and know I have to slay this creature. I awaken in terror.*

In analysis, the dreamer associated the pale blue eyes to her boss. "Oh my goodness," she exclaimed, "Those are just like P.'s eyes, that steely blue that stares straight through a person." She saw the eyes as an element of intimidation he could wield over her, controlling her with fear about her marriage, her career and her finances. As soon as she came into my office she announced, "I don't care if we go bankrupt, I am leaving that job. It is not a place I can go to anymore, it is dangerous for me spiritually and emotionally. I don't want to have an affair with this man. I want to work on my marriage."

She left the job. Whether or not her life situation improved, given the story her dream was telling her, it was essential for her to assert herself. In our discussion about the dream, the conversation was more like show and tell, rather than search and explore. She knew what the dream presented in the way of taking action. I was there to support her and listen.

Here is another dream that was clear upon awakening, and changed a person's life:

> *I dreamed I moved to Coppell, died and went to heaven. I'm a workaholic; in my mind, God wears a suit, like a businessman. And now I'm expecting this great job in heaven, because I'm a good worker. Instead, God shakes his head sadly. "WHAT?!" And the answer I hear is, "When I needed you most, you bailed out, you left."*[1]

The situation had to do with a real estate developer moving to the "safe" suburbs of Dallas, forsaking his homeland, Oak Cliff, a hilly and ethnically diverse older neighborhood near downtown Dallas. Even though he had extreme difficulty finding a bank to finance his renewal projects, since the dream he has spent twelve years renovating interesting architectural gems in his old neighborhood, thereby helping to create a major transformation in Oak Cliff. He reported that his vivid dream changed his life's course from that day forward.

Exercise: Sharing Life Altering Dreams

If members of your dream group have had life-altering dreams that caused them to feel certain of what the dreams were directing them to do, share those with each other now. As each member shares, the group is to provide support, and to witness, no more and no less.

---

1 Anon., *Dallas Morning News*, "Sunday Life," Feb. 5, 2006. p. 14

Complexes – the Hidden Gold[1]

Pull out your notebook and a good pen. Spend some time relaxing and centering yourselves. Agree jointly that your space will be protected from harm and dedicated to consciousness. Have one member who enjoys doing it "talk" the group into a safe, comfortable, deep place by reading the following aloud:

Close your eyes and go back in time a week or two, perhaps to when we all were together last, and think of an unpleasant experience. Knowing that it is sometimes natural, even healthy to forget or deny dark times deep inside, let your memory wander until you discover an experience that will help you understand how your complexes are triggered. It could be an event in which you felt very angry, or deeply sad or hurt. Perhaps you were frustrated and wanted to shout and scream; perhaps you were embarrassed because someone mocked you for pouting. You might even have wanted to do something cruel to get back at someone.

(Pause)

When you have seen and felt that event, write it down in your notebook. Include all possible detail: How did you feel? Did your feelings match the event or could they have been an overreaction? Can you identify the old, familiar feeling that came up in this experience? When did you feel like this in childhood? What were the circumstances? What was the essential life experience that shaped your sensitivity in this area?

1 See: Jung, "A Review of The Complex Theory," in "The Structure and Dynamics of the Psyche," *Collected Works*, Vol. 8, p. 92

What you have identified in this exercise is a complex.[1] You will be able to recognize it in the future, and when you are grabbed by it, you will know that you are not operating from your mature personality, but rather from the wounded small self that still leaps into being on occasion. Usually it is wise to back away from conflict or fall silent when a complex is hit. It can help to avoid many of the apologies you would otherwise want to make later on.

If the group wishes, you might share about this exercise. Understand that these experiences are often very upsetting and humbling for the waking self to take in, and if there is sharing, real sensitivity and respect are in order. One must not shame, commiserate, or display other judgments, because as you will see in the following journal entry, as well as the next chapter, such actions only indicate that judging and being judged are closely linked.

Here is an example of some work on complexes an older male physician has generously donated to this workbook:

I went to the hospital the other day to have some tests taken before I was scheduled to go in for a hernia repair At the elevator, I stood next to a woman dressed in street clothes who was carrying a stuffed animal. A nurse walked by and spoke to the woman – evidently they knew each other and worked together. The nurse expressed surprise to see her, and I soon realized that it was the woman's day off. My elevator companion mumbled something about needing to visit a patient on the children's unit. It seemed she was a nurse too, and was there to visit and bring a gift to a patient. Immediately, I hated her and was furious with her. How dare she think she is so important that she has to schlep back to the hospital on her day off just to see a patient and bring a gift, as though she is a real family member! And such a martyr! Doesn't she already see the patient about 40+ hours a week? What a grandiose big shot.

Then I decided to examine this little scene, since it did seem a bit of an overreaction to hate a woman for visiting a sick child. I determined that it was her self-importance and her lack of attention to her own life and her

1 For more on complexes, see *Threads, Knots, Tapestries*, p. 21

own needs that was getting to me. Whether this was really the case for her or not, it was the case for me. Right away I saw how I was just like her – filled with martyrdom and Mother Teresa bullshit. The only way I can get any validity at all is when I am taking care of others, when I am going to absurd lengths to accommodate my own patients. Years ago I went to the rape crisis telephone line to do my shift when the city was shut down by an ice storm. The director called me when she heard I had driven in and taken the shift, admonishing me and saying I had no business risking my life like that. She was pretty horrified that I would go to such lengths. I told myself it was about responsibility and commitment, but it really was about getting approval and buying love.

The complex is related to my mother. I had to care for her, as many children care for their disabled parents. She was insecure, so I told her she was pretty. She had to work, so to help her, I did many more chores than any of my friends did at their homes. She liked Ed Sullivan, so I watched it with her. When "White Christmas" came on the radio at Christmas time, I would turn it up and dance with glee, not because it was my favorite Christmas song, but because it was hers. I don't think I knew then – and maybe don't know even now – what I'd call my favorite Christmas song. I realized, from this flash of judgmental irritation at a total stranger, that I had exactly the problem I was projecting onto her – a need to buy love and approval from any source, because I hadn't any inside. And it is up to me now to discover myself and have the courage to live my life, not to live in service to others, even though that may sound really selfish.

The journal entry shows us a person who was thoughtful about an emotional reaction that seemed extreme. It provided him an opportunity to discover a nest of trouble in his psyche, one he can substantially heal with more consciousness.

Complexes will manifest in dream group both through dreams and in the relationships among its members. A complex in a dream often feels threatening, like hearing a person breaking into your house, or trying to brake a car that only keeps rolling backwards, and similar images. (Keep in mind that the complex would have to be determined by the dreamer's associations, and that the dream images cited are not necessarily images of complexes.) One will find that dreams regularly comment on our complexes being triggered by offering exaggerated images to point out, in vivid color, our emotional overkill. Usually complexes beat us up pretty badly, for the negative self-talk can be quite debilitating. Complexes can disturb those around us as well. When we are in a complex, our friends and family may well be quite annoyed with us. If I have millions of dollars, but won't commit to a vacation with you because I tell you I am worried about money, you might reasonably be a bit pissed off. Most attacks by complexes arouse exasperation, rather than solicitations of pity and understanding. While comfort may be the response one most wants in this situation, it is the least likely reaction to appear. Hyperbole in dreams often suggests a complex is at hand.

In all dream circles, some relationships will form and some will fall apart. The complexes and issues we project onto others are prime factors in this ambivalent outcome. Dreams, however, give us a chance to see our issues from a different perspective. Too often, we view the world through tunnel vision that is focused on the ego's demands and not only lacks empathy, but is devoted to confirming each and every prejudice we have had since childhood. I urge all dream circles to be as empathic and conscious as possible in dealing with relationships within the group. Please push yourselves to find the less obvious factors in any conflict before you take action on your anger. Groups that can deal with thorny, sensitive material and remain safe and trusting groups are rare. Your circle can succeed if each person commits to a level of support beyond what they have previously experienced.

Exercise

Find dreams that touch complexes in you, and take turns sharing this in your dream circle. What insights did you gain from the exercise? How did it feel to share that somewhat embarrassing material? What can be done to cope with the complex so that it does not run roughshod over your life?

The Shadow

The Shadow is a central Jungian concept because it is universally pertinent as a psychological insight. Simply put, there is a whole lot about all of us of which we are unaware. Worse, some of it tends to be unflattering, and worse yet, you are more likely to see mine before I do. Let's jump in before this notion gets too disturbing.

EXERCISE: ME AND MY SHADOW

List ten people who annoy you. They need to be the same sex as you are. If you are gay or transgender, you might want to use the gender with which you most identify. Do *not* use any members of dream group, or any people the group all knows. You may use actresses, newscasters, and other well-known people you do not know personally. Do not use your sister- or brother-in-law; this is an exercise in projection, not relationship. Try to stay away from politics, because that form of projection is a collective one and difficult to use satisfactorily in this exercise. A neighbor you don't know well but rather dislike would be a good choice, for example.

Write what you dislike about these ten people. Describe the exact behaviors you dislike or judgments about them (s/he is a phony) that irritate you. Then describe how you can see the identical issues in yourself. Finally, list what you envy about the people who irritate you.

It is not true in every single instance, but the vast majority of our shadow projections are actually about envy. Think of all the times the boss is hated and criticized. Think about how often Tyra Banks, Jessica Simpson and Oprah Winfrey and their body-weight has been on public display – all to the enjoyment and satisfaction of the audience. Being human, we tend to disparage the very people we most want to resemble.

What is so wonderful about envy is that you can use it to improve yourself. If you envy a neighbor who is a partner in a downtown law firm, then take a look at your own career, goals, education and ambition. You might not drop everything and go to law school, but you could look for a better job, or ask for a promotion. Envy is an arrow that points us in a particular direction that we are unconsciously interested in taking. Experiment with using envy as a guidepost.

List all of the envy points you can imagine: I am envious of his sailboat; I am envious of her ability to speak in front of an audience; I am envious that he says his sex life is so exciting, and so on.

Next, make a to-do list for yourself. Some things cannot be changed: if you are 40 and envy a 20-year-old, there isn't much you can do to change into a younger person. But there may be other actions to take – entering therapy or analysis is a possibility, or living in a loft, or taking a rafting trip down the Colorado River in the Grand Canyon. What, exactly, is youth? What does it mean to you? If you deconstruct the notion of youth, what options does your life offer that you can still give yourself?

The beginning of the list might look like this:

Quit smoking
Finish my degree
Make more friends
Exercise more
Laugh more often

Spend more time with my family

Now you know more about where your energy lies, where there is passion for change. This list comes from the inside out, not the outside in; it points to new paths to be successful.

To make this exercise a bit more personal and immediate, try this next step.

EXERCISE: I ENVY YOU FOR . . .

Ask each member to write on a tablet how the other members are enviable. Write down one envied quality for each member of the group, and when everyone is finished, share your answers with each other.

Jane: *I envy your long, beautiful hair.*

Joe: *I envy your relationship with your wife.*

Mary: *I envy your relationship with the facilitator of this group; it seems to me you are the favorite.*

Ideally, with each statement of envy, the listener will have eye contact, nod and acknowledge the envy.

After each person has completed the first step by sharing points of envy with each member of dream group, as well as being the recipient of other members' comments, rewrite the statements on your tablets to include compliments followed by action items. It will probably take some time to think through how your feeling of envy can be transmuted into praise and positive action. Then go around the circle again:

Jane: *I love your long beautiful hair, and I have decided to let mine grow a bit.*

Joe: *I respect your relationship with your wife and am setting the goal of meeting new people before our next dream group.*

Mary: *I think your relationship with the facilitator is terrific, and this week I am going to look at my need to win the approval of authorities. I commit to writing (or meditating on, making a collage of, capturing the feeling in a photo, writing a poem about it, etc.) about this issue before our next meeting.*

Dealing with envy in this way is healing. Hating goodness in people is neither productive nor compassionate, but using envy for your own growth of consciousness is healthy and practical.

This time, each member can acknowledge the compliment with eye contact and a nod, or a "thank you," if that is what feels best. Don't forget, the shadow is simply unconscious matter that generally wants to come up for air. Each and every negative feeling one has toward another is a shadow issue that can potentially be made conscious. Once that's done, it will very likely cease to irritate you.

Imagine what would happen to wars if we looked at conflict this way. Countries, or at least their leaders, have shadow projections just as do individuals, families and communities.

Dreams and the Shadow

Now you are ready to look at shadow figures in your dreams. Each time you dream about someone, whether you recognize the figure or not, you have dreamed an element of your shadow, something unconscious that is projected onto another figure by way of gaining your attention, focusing your energy so some change can happen.

Exercise: Shadow Role Play

In this exercise, dramatic skills and talents are the focus and vehicle through which one can tap into his or her shadow material in a more complete way than can be accomplished by merely talking about it.

Begin by selecting one of those shadow behaviors that most disgusts you. Go back to the qualities you despise on the list of characters you made (exploitative, arrogant, manipulative, etc.) – in this case, the worse, the better. Then, using a scenario from recent memory, construct a short vignette to act out. Cast dream group members as your players, give them direction, and then play your shadow to the hilt. Exaggerate, just as dreams do to make the point. If you are catty, gossipy, competitive, a cheat or a liar, exaggerate that – be a monster at it. Let yourself feel the role, act it out and make it conscious. This can be a very freeing, enlightening experience. But fair warning: this exercise is not for those who lack spiritual courage.

Shadow in Dream Group

It is quite likely, even desirable, for dream group members to begin dreaming about each other. Invariably, shadow projections become part of the gooey, sticky mix of a dream circle. Remember: with respect, patience and by refraining from judgment, groups can weather just about anything, even conflict, dislike, and shadow projection.

Jealousy is one of the first and most important issues in dream group and shadow work. If your dream circle was able to complete the previous exercise on envy, then you have made an important step forward.

At this point, it is a good idea to recall the rules about not talking about group outside the group meetings. It is imperative that there be no discussion about any individual's issue(s) outside the dream circle; all of the relationship material needs to stay in the group.

"But what if two of us go out to lunch and want to talk about our friendship, are we to do that only in front of the other group members?" No, that is an example of a direct line of communication – two people, their only agenda being each other. The problem would exist if they went out to lunch and discussed a third person from the group; such gossip is unfair, and will lead to a group that can be weakened or, eventually, even destroyed.

Triangulation

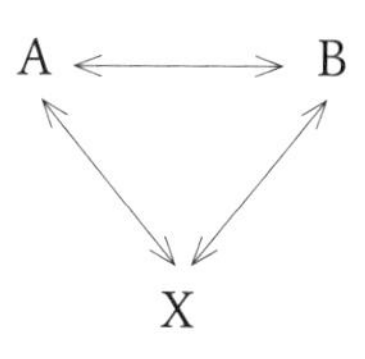

Triangulation is a *very* important minefield to understand and avoid. If I have a problem with you and speak to you about it, that is a direct line of communication between the two of us. If instead, I go to a third person to talk or complain about you, I have then created a triangle by discussing you with another.

This causes difficulties in dream group (or any family or collection of people), because members are not admitting shadow projections onto each other. Avoiding such talk is a rule that has to be established in order for the group to feel safe and grow together. When you are tempted to break the rule, even just a little bit, know that you will build a stronger foundation and connection to the Self if you resist and refuse to voice your thoughts. Look at your thoughts as either material that you need to make conscious in yourself (shadow stuff), or an issue that you need to bring to the group because it is interfering with your work together.

Shadow Mask Exercise

As with dream dolls, it can be meaningful and fulfilling to give the time and effort to produce a piece of art – in this case a mask based on the psychological work the group has accomplished from this chapter. Simply render in artistic form the face of your shadow. We know the shadow is unconscious, so bringing this part of our psyche into the light of day is potent, but often difficult. Keep in mind that when one works to manifest unconscious insights in the waking, physical world, the effort will be rewarded. Though it cannot be predicted or guaranteed, it is my observation that few are ever disappointed when they do their best to bring forth their shadow mask. This activity can be accomplished in several ways. Here are a few possibilities:

The hand-held flat mask: using cardboard, cut out a flat shape that will allow the artist to hold the mask up to her face when it is attached to a dowel or popsicle stick. Decorate the cardboard with paints, crayon, pastels, glitter, feathers, tissue paper, fabric, photographs, or anything your imagination desires. A paper plate will work, too, for a quick, uncomplicated project.

The papier maché mask: using wire mesh or wadded newspapers and masking tape, create a form on which to drape wet strips of newsprint dipped in papier maché mix. Using layers (which most likely will have to be made in several steps, allowing drying time in between), the artist creates the three dimensional shape of a face. It can be as grotesque, funny or realistic as he desires. The last layer of papier maché needs to be plain newsprint or white tissue paper, unless it's desired that print or other patterns show through to the final product. When the molding process is complete and fully dry, paint the mask to finish the project. Finally, spray the mask with several coats of fixative to achieve a glossy, finished look. Two holes can be punched into the sides by the ears so that the mask can be worn or hung on a wall.

The paper bag mask: cut out eye, nose and mouth holes in a large paper bag to make a mask that fits over the entire head. If the bag has unwanted printing on it, it can be opened up, reversed and glued or taped back together. Again, using paint, colored and/or handmade papers, oil crayons, spray paint, etc., decorate the bag to represent the shadow self.

The plaster of Paris mask: pour plaster of Paris mix – about enough to make a dinner plate sized circle – onto a large sheet of wax paper. Make a loop of heavy twine and insert it at the top of the pool of plaster so the mask will hang on the wall when it is dry. While it is wet, insert items that will form the face. (When it's dry, the imbedded items will not fall out.) Items can be rocks, crystals, leaves, twigs, straw, shells, paper clips, jewelry, marbles, broken glass, dried beans, hair clippings, etc. One mask-maker used amethysts for her eyes, straw for her hair, a shell for her nose and cranberries for her mouth. The mask represented the wild woman shadow element she had repressed. The plaster mask is one to display or hang, rather than wear.

These are just a few suggestions; the group can think "outside the box," and come up with other ways to implement this project. Each person could choose to make a mask using a different method, or the group could gather all of the materials and devote one session to making the masks together. Dedicate a dream circle session to sharing your creations and processing the experience. Some questions for discussion might be:

- What name can you give to your shadow?
- Where does this shadow cause you problems in life?
- How can this shadow element help you?
- What would it be like to integrate your shadow?

Take some time now to look back and reflect. You have looked at shadow, complexes, your childhood dream-self, and many other elements. What have you learned? What do you need or want to learn? How would you describe your process now?

Scapegoats

Sometimes one person – perhaps the leader, perhaps someone else – will become a scapegoat. This is a tribal group reality that needs to be made conscious as quickly as possible. What is the person who is being singled out carrying for the group?

These are some scapegoating trends I have seen over the years:

1. A person who is far more conservative than the rest of the group will be scapegoated. In effect, that person carries the shadow of the members who are unconscious about their own conservative nature, and projects it onto others in a disparaging manner. We would all benefit from admitting that, in terms of the political divide in the United States, we are more muddled than we think. A person who thought gay people disgusting, a woman who sold makeup for a living and a well-to-do matron who came to dream group terribly over-dressed were all victims of group scorn. These judgments must somehow be addressed, rather than covered up and talked about later. If you are adamant that gay people need to be treated with respect, you will have to speak your truth and confront whatever intolerance you perceive. But you also would do well to declare yourself intolerant and reflect on that part of yourself. Intolerance of intolerance is still intolerance.

2. A person who hogs the time or rambles on about mundane issues will end up being scapegoated. However, it's a lot cleaner and less destructive to own your anger and say, "I find myself angry with you, because it seems that you take more time than other

members." Or simply, "I want to focus on dreams". That might lead to a discussion about making the process more democratic, dividing the time, or even drawing names or taking turns. It is also an opening for the person taking more than his or her share of time to see what that complex is about. Perhaps that type of behavior happens outside of group and turns other people off, too. It's possible the rambler could be avoiding something important. Maybe the "time hog" would benefit from discovering where the hogging originated, how it developed in his or her personality, and how it might be resolved. Anger is usually fertile if we let it lead to mature, conscious behavior and not let it sit until it festers into resentment. But this cannot be a gang rape. It is inappropriate for other members to jump into agreement and say, "Me too!" It is a one-to-one exchange, and the person brave enough to voice the confrontation must resist encouraging a lynch mob mentality, no matter how tempting that may be.

Unfortunately, the leader (unless it is she who is being scapegoated) is often the one who caused the problem. Classroom teachers, choir directors and office managers are all human, and always tend to find one or two people who will collect their displeasure like magnets; clearly, the leader is projecting shadow onto the person who "is irritating." The dream circle or class is apt to follow the lead of that teacher, because subtle clues can induce a group into thinking it is acceptable to scapegoat another in their group. It is essential that the leader take charge in an enlightened way, treat each member with dignity and fairness, and not allow unconscious projections to take possession of her group.

It is human nature to scapegoat, which suggests we have developed these habits and behaviors to survive and thrive. Nonetheless, they are negative, selfish and destructive attitudes. Thinking oneself superior to another is an attitude that encompasses nearly all of our problems. Scapegoating is simply wanting to distance oneself from those whose qualities we deem to be inferior or immoral, or whom we judge simply because we can't bear to own those qualities ourselves. It is about protecting our power and maintaining a closed, unthreatened system.

Exercise

Use the time to open a discussion about your group dynamics. Each person can answer these questions:

How included or excluded do you feel?
Who would you like to know better?
How safe do you feel in dream circle?

Please use responsible "I" statements, not "you" statements. For example, say, "I feel left out," rather than, " . . . . you make me feel left out." Take time to process this exercise. Was it difficult? Frightening? Was it a release? How has your group changed after discussing the dynamics?

The Masculine/Feminine Principal in Dreams

Regarding the opposite sex of dream figures, approach this as your deepest, most difficult work. This is where God is found, in the layers of the psyche that defy rational understanding and refuse to sanction our comfort zones or support our status quo. We are challenged by dream material, ergo the reason so many people discount or ignore our sacred inner stories and poetry. There is a man in each woman, and there is a woman in each man. (And yes, there are women in women and men in men, as was discussed in the last chapter on shadow projection.) But the opposite gender projection is different from the others, and is not in the least subject to gender sensitivities. Let's open our minds a bit and admit that, for the most part, nature divided us into two distinct categories, and it is an ancient part of our brains that is genetically, socially and relationally aligned this way. And since the majority of us are one gender and not the other, whether gay or straight, we project "other" onto the gender we are not. Transgender persons are controversial and often draw hate from insensitive and close-minded people, because fiddling with this most primal of divisions seems wrong, perverted, unnatural, and therefore frightening.

Actually, transgender people appear in the literature of ancient cultures, and are also reported in anthropological studies of various groups. Hermaphroditus was a Greek God. As a boy, he was merged with the nymph Salmacis, who was so enamored of him she prayed that, "the twain might become one flesh."[1] Hermaphroditus was the son of Hermes, the messenger of the Gods, and Aphrodite, the ultimate woman, and in recent history we referred to a person with both sets of genitalia as an hermaphrodite. Although that term is currently considered pejorative, male/female identity-gender roles and gay/straight/bisexuality are a complex mix of endless possibilities and descriptive terms, which are found throughout history and cross-culturally.

For example, in the days before the reservations, the Lakota had a place in their culture for men to live as women. A man who wanted to be married to a man was accepted; he would stay with the women and perform their chores with them while the men went on hunts or to war. On the other hand, I have researched a Lakota woman who was called Clown Woman.[2] She was a legendary chief, leader, shaman and warrior of the Lakota.

Gender is a guideline or a focal point, not a firm fact. Many of you have probably noticed how women become more masculine as they age, and men more feminine in their later years. Women's juices tend to get flowing around 50, when they might produce their most courageous and important work. Likewise, men tend to become softer, even sentimental, in old age.

Jung characterized the concept of the contra-sexual, and the coming to awareness of a feminine presence within the male and a masculine presence within the female as some of the most important work of the psyche. This chapter is devoted to several exercises that touch on that concept, in hopes that some of the numinosity of this inner journey will begin to draw the reader and dreamer into this curious and wonderful realm.

1 Kenney, *Metamorphoses*, Ovid, iv, 347
2 Castleman, *Religious Traditions of the Lakota Sioux and How They Relate to Analytical Psychology (Diploma Thesis)*

Exercise: Being Born the Opposite Gender

As is always the case, this exercise will be as significant for you as the amount of effort you put into it. If you find yourself saying, "Well nothing would be different if I were born the opposite sex," you will know that either you have not delved deeply enough into your imagination, or you are resistant to what insights might surface in the exercise. Please take some time now to relax in the dream group, to center. Close your eyes and mentally go to some favorite place in nature, find a hole and crawl into it. Let that hole represent your deep unconscious, your creative dream-maker, a wellspring of thought, insight and imagination – in a word, the underworld. Now ever so slowly, see yourself changing just one of the circumstances of your life: your gender. You are now born … … (fill in the sex). Look to see the reactions of your parents. What happens to the family dynamics when you are born in this new gender? How does it affect the feelings of your siblings, grandparents, and so on? Now walk through the course of your life. What are the first few years like? How different is the beginning of school? Isn't it likely that your interests would be different? Where might your talents be encouraged and developed? Take it slowly, viewing your life as a film-maker would record a documentary. What toys do you love most? How different are your friends? What if you (women) had been given only trucks and guns, or (men) only dolls and tea sets on your birthdays? (Even if your parents were forward thinking, society isn't.) Each day, and in every way, you would be perceived in a manner opposite from your history. Think about being outside, playing during school recess. Where would you be on the playground, and what would you be doing?

Next, move into adolescence. What is this like for you? What activities might you develop a special interest in now? Who would your friends be? How would you dress? Who might you have a crush on? (Those of you who are gay, try this exercise remaining gay; later, if you wish, you can do it the other way.) What would sports be like? As you develop socially, what kind of romantic partner are you? What are your favorite subjects in school? What do you like to watch on television, and what are your favorite books? (For women: when a boy socks you in the stomach after school, what do you do?) (For men: when the girls gossip about you in the bathroom, and spread a rumor that you're "fast," how do you feel?) Follow your imagination in this fashion, being as creatively thorough as you can be.

Move on to college or the working world now. How have your interests changed? What your career do you choose? As a lover, what kind of partner do you favor? How would sex be? How would you make love if you were the opposite sex? Who are the people to whom you are sexually attracted? What would be your preferences in dress, hair, jewelry and automobiles? What hobbies would you choose? And finally, what is your name?

Now slowly open your eyes and come back to the dream circle. Record in a journal, or a laptop, just what you experienced. Along with describing what your imagination showed you, add how you felt in this exercise: where did you find resistance, difficulty, delight, sadness, pleasure or any other feeling, insight, thought, or sensation? Finally, share with the dream circle some of what you've discovered. You can, Of course, choose to share only those parts with which you are comfortable. But on the whole, talking together about the process helps each member to clarify just which valuable aspects in our personalities are lost due to social gender standards.

Photograph Exercise

Equipment: Digital camera, photo paper, opposite sex clothing, jewelry, hair gel, fake mustaches or beards, wigs, hats for both sexes and make-up.

First, have each member take a head shot (in black and white) as s/he normally looks. This is a self-portrait, not a posed Christmas card glamour shot. Then put on opposite sex clothing, fixing your hair and accessories to look the way you would if you had been born the opposite gender. Now take the head shot again – same distance from the camera, same backdrop, same lighting and same black and white contrast.

Print both shots on photo paper. Mount them side by side; you can double mat them, print them side by side on one sheet of photo paper, or paste both photos on a larger sheet as a collage or self-portrait.

Now process the discoveries that turned up in the exercise, and look at your creations. What do you see? How does it feel? What kind of memories, feelings of loss, wishes and fears does this stir in you? What parts were uncomfortable? Which differences were surprising? What did you learn about yourself? What dreams can you recall that might have elements of this personality you have uncovered? *Which man or woman you know most represents who you think you would be, if you were the opposite gender?*

Why do you suppose this exercise might be uncomfortable? Can you imagine more than one reason? Try to perceive the issue from the perspective of consciousness: why do I feel so "icky" or "guilty" or (fill in the blank) when I imagine myself as the opposite sex? Here are some examples of journal entries to help you get started:

When I first saw anything that resembled a homosexual act, it was in a park and I was about fourteen years old. This was a long time ago. Homosexuality was never mentioned openly at home or among my friends. "Queer" was a term used in junior high school as a generic put down of those who seemed odd.

What I saw was a group of men together. One of them was in drag – he had balloons under his tight t-shirt and the ends of the balloons served as the nipples. He had on a platinum wig, and was rubbing his chest on the other men's chests and making sexual remarks and noises. They men grabbed his balloon breasts and laughed. They saw me, and that egged them on. They said things like, "Hey little girl, I guess you've never seen a real woman have you? Well here is one, so take a good look." As you can imagine, it terrified me, but I was fascinated as well. Then he propped his leg up on one of the stone benches they were gathered around, and pretended to be shaving his legs, all the while giving me a verbal commentary. I got out of there fast.

This image stayed in my mind for a long time and really haunted me. Now I understand it better, but even so, they were being mean to me, trying to scare me. That feeling is what comes up when I try this exercise, even though being the opposite sex has nothing to do with that group of gay men in the park so long ago. But at some deep level, it feels wrong or weird or scary or sickening. I think this exercise is difficult because I am so embarrassed by this homophobic-sounding memory, but I have it and cannot make it go away.

Here one finds an honest attempt to review a painful and confusing memory that had colored her feelings about cross-dressing and the world of ambiguous sexuality. A second journal contribution from another analysand:

When I looked at myself in the black and white photos, it really freaked me out. I felt a little sad, too. It seems like there is so much life, so many possibilities I missed by being born a man. While in the past, I disparaged things like women's magazines, I realized through this exercise that I have missed so much, like my mom teaching me how to cook, how to sew, and all the feminine mysteries of make-up and conversation. I actually don't feel women puzzle me as much as before I tried this. That is really hard to admit to myself. It is okay for women to do manly things, but unacceptable for a man to crochet?

And finally, from a woman:

I really saw myself as a man. I would wear a ponytail, dress in black, and own an art gallery. I would have sex with as many women as I could, without making a commitment. I would want to be free to explore my sexuality without any guilt. I would collect edgy and fascinating art. People would think of me as an iconoclast, yet I would have some clout in the community.

Participants often get in touch with some sense of loss in this exercise. When we conjure up the person of the opposite sex, we may realize it is a part of us that has never been allowed to exist. Yet in dreams, we are both men and women. We find personalities in us, parts of us that are compelling, confusing, shocking, exciting and stimulating. We can integrate these aspects figuratively, if not in a literal way, but the work of integrating the contrasexual aspect is all about allowing more of the disowned facets of ourselves to be re-owned, to be brought to use and fulfillment.[1]

1 Recommended reading: Eugenides, *Middlesex*

Dealing with more … Difficulties

There are so many ways to encounter difficulties that this subject alone could fill several volumes and still not cover all the ways trouble can be handled. Only the essentials of dealing with problems can be covered in this small chapter, so I must appeal to the group's common sense and wisdom. In other words, be adult, and do not do to others what you would not want done to you. [1]

With that counsel, here are some specific situations that might arise in which a review of rules and guidelines would be essential.

When emotions escalate to yelling and name-calling.

When a member literally runs out of the group.

When a member terminates abruptly, either by phone or by not showing up again.

A few rules:

1. Do not speak for anyone but yourself. Do not take on anyone else's opinions or emotions.

If you want to comment, try this: "When I heard George yelling at Paul, I felt sick and scared, just as I did when my parents fought," rather than, "You two shouldn't fight like this in dream circle."

---

1 According to the Gospel of Thomas and some religious scholars, Jesus said, "Do not do unto others as you would not have them do unto you." It seems to me that while an act of kindness is a good thing, in the scope of human relationships, avoiding cruelty is at least as important.

Or you could say: "I am really concerned about Paul and what he must be feeling right now," not, "I know Paul is upset," or, "Since he is so upset, let's stop the group right now."

A paradoxical rule of dream work in group is that during difficult exchanges, the only person you need to be concerned about is yourself. The rest of the emotion in the room is not about you, does not reflect on you and, in an odd way, is none of your business. Each member has a right to feel or think whatever s/he feels or thinks, period. There are boundaries: I am me, you are you, and if you don't like me that is more about you than it's about me. I do not have to own it as my personal material, or make it a judgment about me.

Here is a simple analogy: chocolate ice cream is a good thing. No one can argue that it is fun and tasty. There is nothing about chocolate ice cream that is intrinsically inferior or lacking. However, for a variety of reasons, not everyone likes chocolate ice cream. Maybe it made one throw up as a child, or it tastes too bitter, or it reminds a person of weight and diet issues. Whatever feeling a person might have about chocolate ice cream does not mean anything about the food itself; it simply is an opinion. And we are all entitled to an opinion. Would you think of making a guest eat something s/he found absolutely unacceptable?

We are similar. We are different. We are what we are. We are chocolate ice cream. For most, we are simply great, unique, even a special treat. For some, whatever their personal reasons, we are not desirable. That is the wheel of life.

Accepting that not everyone will like me is a challenge. Not wanting to change to be something that would make me more acceptable is a challenge. Not changing my insides to fit someone else's outside is a challenge.

2. Maintain the third position: if difficulty arises, it is imperative that each dream group member remain centered, focused,

conscious and aware of her or his feelings as a spectator, not as a participant.

Perhaps a few examples will illustrate this point:

Do not say, "I hate you, you are mean, you are cruel, you are judgmental, you are hiding your feelings, you are defensive, you are hurting this group," or other negative comments you might be tempted to voice.

Say instead, "I feel anger when I listen to you." "I feel pain when I listen to you." "I feel like protecting myself when I listen to you." "I feel scared when I listen to you, afraid our group might fall apart." "I wonder, is something important not being said, or is that feeling something that is entirely about me?"

Here is the really tricky part:

Since I am aware of a tribal unconscious, and have written a book about the places where we overlap in our psyches, communication in dream group is even more complicated. I have my feelings; they are about my history, my genetics, my karma and my personality. They are mine and mine alone.

You have your feelings, so that is just as true for you.

We have a relationship. Those are the feelings we share; they are in the space between us. Think of how infrequently we truly fall in love in our lifetimes,[1] perhaps about three times. Does this imply that the odds are three in six billion that the person you fall in love with will love you, too? If love did not create a mutual field, I don't think our species would have multiplied as well as it has. Our animal sex drive would have produced babies, but the importance of living in family and clans cannot be denied as essential for the survival of a human being. It was by necessity that we loved and formed relationships, which are reciprocal to some degree. True, it doesn't happen all of the time, but on occasion they are magical, fantastic communal experiences beyond any rational explanation. There simply is shared space between us that is mutual – it is ours.

---

1 Hendrix, *Getting the Love You Want: A Guide for Couples*

So we have us. Defining *us*, as opposed to all of the projections *we* put on *you* is very sophisticated business, and is something of which dream group helps people to become aware.

Exercise

Add to my rules. There can be many, or only one or two more, depending on the needs and personalities in the dream circle. Do you need to put conflict in writing before you discuss it? Do you need each person to commit to staying with the group even when angry? Discuss such ideas, and make an agreement between yourselves about how you will handle conflict, and which rules are the most essential for your group to follow.

Part Six

The Sacred Circle

photo: Michael N. Geh

My Dream, Your Dream, or Both?

In this chapter we will focus on two kinds of dreams: first, dreams in which members of dream group play characters in other members' dreams, and second, dreams that seem universal, or at least linked thematically to some or all of the members of the group. In the case of thematic dreams, they actually can become material for others to experience. In this instance, *each person can make the dream material that is discussed his or her dream, even though she did not actually dream it.* This is not the same as telling the dreamer what you think the dream means, but rather, taking the dream as your own, as if you dreamt it yourself. This sounds very like the popular statement used in dream groups, "If it were my dream . . . . .," but it isn't the same at all. One major difference is that other circle members do not talk about their own process until the dreamer is *completely* finished exploring her dream. The second difference is that it is not "If it were my dream," but rather, "Because this is truly my dream." or "The work you have shared on your dream has touched me, because I, too, have loneliness," for example.

But let's begin with the kind of dream in which members of our dream group actually appear in a dream. That may not have happened yet, but over time, it almost certainly will.

These are some of the most interesting, enjoyable and challenging dreams to work on in the group setting. It is essential that all participants are interested in working from a trusting, conscious place in the psyche, as well as having the sense that the group is healing and helpful, not destructive or cruel. It is not possible to overstate the importance of compassion, because the likelihood of getting an open and vulnerable person to forgive and forget an unkind remark is nearly zero.

Let's begin with a dream in which one member, some members, or even all members of the dream group appear. First, the dream is processed just as the group would work with any dream. The dreamer tells the dream in detail, associates to each image (all of the characters in the dream), gives the dream a title, states the plot and setting, describes the mood and tone of the dream and anything else that seems relevant. Here is where the tricky part comes in: if I dream about a member of the group, that means I have to state freely and honestly my associations to that member. Maybe I am jealous of her (shadow projection), or maybe I judge her for some of her ideals. Perhaps she has been catty, or maybe someone said she was talking about me behind my back (one cardinal rule of dream group is not to talk behind someone's back), and now the dream has brought all of that to the surface. If nothing else, dreams will, over time, reveal the sort of stuff that is lurking within, and which we would rather not reveal. Ideally the dreamer will be honest yet compassionate. Considering the dream's importance for the whole group, the dreamer may have to disclose unfavorable feelings toward the member who is the subject of the dream. Even if the feelings are entirely positive, the purpose of dream associations requires that we expose our innermost feelings.

It can go something like this:

I dreamed about C. walking through mud with big, heavy, rubber boots on her feet. What I associate to C. is that she is really strong, powerful; she knows her way, and she is forceful. I think that is a part of me I need to develop. I could learn from her. Sometimes her opinions are more than I want to hear, but I respect her for being on target almost all of the time. I think she is invincible in some ways. I think she really can wade through the muck of life and get through hard times. I am going through a hard time

right now with both of my parents being ill, and I think C is that driving, determined part of me that my dream says can get me through hard times.
Or it may go something like this:

I dreamed that G was in the group, running around wildly and making faces and yelling. She made the faces by stretching out her lips with her fingers while putting her face right in other's faces in an aggressive way. It was very unsettling, and I woke up in a rage.

I have thought a lot about this dream, and though it really frightens me to share it with the group, I also don't want to avoid sharing it. I think G is a shadow projection for me. I see qualities in her that I don't care for, but may need to find in myself. Sometimes I think she is aggressive, loud, opinionated and bossy. I know this is probably my own stuff, but that is what I make up about G. I also think she is really creative, surprising, brave and wild. She embodies a wild woman energy that I know I have had to struggle with, because it scares me and yet I want it, too.

At this point, the group could ask G how she feels about what the dreamer has risked volunteering. G might be hurt, flattered, angry, excited or frightened. She might say:

Well, I appreciate that you have been honest with me, and with the group, by bringing this up. I can be wild, and sometimes I am too aggressive, so I think your dream about me is accurate. I think I've frightened a lot of people in my life, and I draw that projection in a lot of relationships.

This is a good example of how the dream about G can be helpful for her, even though it was another member's dream. But it is also worth noting that G need not take it too personally, as the dream had more to do with the dreamer than with her.

Years ago, a colleague called to tell me she'd had a dream about me: "I dreamed you were trying to steal my silver spoons." She thought it indicated something terrible about me, so she was calling to warn me that her dream had revealed something secret and awful. I can be secretive, and certainly am frequently awful, but I don't believe the dream was as literal as she thought. Since I have the advantage of years of perspective about our relationship, and since the friend died long ago, I think it is safe to say that the dream had little, if anything, to do with me. But it unquestionably had a great deal to do with our relationship, and this is what we can learn from dreams about people we love and hate. They present relationship issues to us, often in the clearest and most embarrassing ways. In this case, the dreamer projected onto to me some aspect that was stealing something precious from her. Stealing can be a metaphor for an unconscious inadequacy and, in fact, the silver spoons were, for her, a symbolic item of great value, the feminine principal.

The dream told her that she feared me, had an unflattering projection on me, and that she had doubts about trusting me. There was also a challenge for me: did her dream tell me accurately of something I needed to see in myself? I'd certainly had a difficult relationship with her, and did not value her age and experience as I might have. I found her a bit controlling, and I am sure I undermined her many times – just like stealing something valuable. I listened to her dream with earnest intent, and that was when our relationship began to improve.

But this kind of awareness needs to come primarily from the dreamer; its importance to the person cast in a role of the dream is of secondary importance. It would be as inappropriate for a dreamer to tell a person portrayed in his dream what the dream means about him or her as it would be for the person depicted in the dream to tell the dreamer what the dream means.

Customarily, after listening carefully, the group can ask questions in order to clarify their understanding of the dream. Then the dreamer has the opportunity to offer her best possible answer to the question, "Why did I need to have this dream?"

The second type of dream is the one that everyone can relate to. Dream circle members may feel a resonance with the dream that marks a sense that personal and collective issues are being touched. The dream might even carry such emotionally strong content that the entire group takes ownership and sees it as a dream for the group.

Dreams of this type show up on a continuum. They may, in amusing ways, be applicable to members in addition to the dreamer, or they may shock each and every group member, and be moving to hear.

Let's look at an example:

> *I see sad, pitiful dogs locked in the kind of cages found at an animal shelter. I try to find a way to help them escape. Finally, a pit bull frees them.*

It actually happened in one dream group session that the image of a bulldog escaping a caged area surfaced in two dreams that were discussed that day. We saw how meaningful that image could be for all of those in the circle, not just the two dreamers. Clearly, when dream images are congruent among two or more members, the tribal field is constellated, and it is important to observe the group process. The tribal field is the area among us that is the sacred dimension manifested in a dream circle. This is where dreams overlap and individuals' processes merge with the group process. Marvin Spiegelman, a respected Jungian analyst who studied with Dr. Jung, refers to this as the "Divine We."[1] Some Jungians feel this is dangerous, that it can contaminate the sacred container of the dream vessel. In other words, people might go a little bonkers with this stuff. All true, no doubt. That is why I have written this handbook, and why this chapter is so near the end of the book. The rules and guidelines presented in the previous chapters are of vital importance in creating a safe dream space, so that bonkers is not what happens, but rather depth, meaning, connection, intimacy, and insight.

The pit bull's escape was an image that meant different things for different members. For some, it was about releasing anger, passion and instinct. For others, the pit bull seemed to be extra-

1 Spiegelman, *The Divine WABA (Within, Among, Between and Around): A Jungian Exploration of Spiritual Paths*

version in avowed introverts; that is, when a lot of energy breaks out of one's comfortable, familiar, public persona (one's cage), it indicates that some deeper, archaic function may need to be given its freedom, i.e., be expressed. Most introverts sit quietly for hours or years thinking, observing, planning and fantasizing. If that goes on too long, when the time comes to express the inner life, it can come out like a tidal wave, crashing over all in its path. Yet letting the pit bull out of the cage is the first step to integration. It is not psychologically healthy to keep parts of ourselves trapped in some prison for all our existence.

One important point to emphasize in this example is the value of not interpreting the pit bull dream simplistically. It would be a quick and dirty path to see this dream as only repressed anger, to give quiet, modest dream group members all sorts of advice about how important it is to express the emotion, and just how to do it. Think of this advice as imperative for you, not the dreamer.

This short dream could be acted out as a psychodrama. I would probably have the dreamer be the dog, and ask another member of the group to "imprison" her by restraining her physically. Emphasizing the sense of imprisonment might bring forth affect or memories that could clarify the dream image far beyond simply releasing anger. We must strive to avoid responses to dreams that are clichés, too pat, too general, or too vague.

Exercise

Select a dream that has resonated for the whole group, and go around the circle, each taking a turn to complete this sentence: "I needed to hear this dream because … ."

Or: "This dream touches my process by … ." Or: "What this dream brings up for me is … ."

Then, as a final step in the exercise, ask the dreamer to state what it was like to hear others in the group react to the dream. Was it invasive? Fascinating? Validating? Frightening? Just listen, letting the dreamer freely explore the complexities of emotion and thought that were evoked by the exercise.

Synchronicity

Synchronicity is described as a meaningful coincidence, or an "acausal connecting principal,"[1] a broad, sweeping definition that includes many paranormal and uncanny events. Others have written extensively on this topic, so it is not my purpose to recapitulate here what has already been written.[2] However, to summarize for our purposes: an acausal connecting principal means that simultaneous events occur that have no discernibly logical relationship. If I turn on the stove, it gets hot; there is a causal relationship between turning the knob and the resulting heat. If I watch a sad movie, I might cry; watching the movie is the event that precipitates the tears. In synchronicity, however, no causal relationship can be detected. No scientific explanation can be given for dreaming about a person you haven't thought of in years and waking the next morning to find an email from this long-lost friend. It is even more compelling to dream about an event that has not yet taken place and find that it eventually does come to pass. Clearly, this defies rational explanation, Newtonian physics and our common understanding of reality.

---

1 Jung, "Synchrony: An Acausal Connecting Principle," *Collected Works*, Vol. 8

2 See: Bolen, *The Tao of Synchronicity;* Jaffé, *An Archetypal Approach to Death Dreams and Ghosts;* and Aziz, *C. G. Jung's Psychology of Religion and Synchronicity.*

Jung was the analytical pioneer who pointed out that such events often have marked psychological meaning. Aniela Jaffé, a close collaborator of Jung's writes:

"Jung has shown that synchronistic, or acausal, phenomena are frequently accompanied by emotions. In an emotional state the level of consciousness is lowered and the contents of the unconscious penetrate the conscious field. We know, however, that the preponderance of the unconscious forms a situation suitable for the occurrence of synchronistic events. The relativity of time and space in the unconscious becomes manifest."[1]

As all groups can, dream circles will manifest emotion exponentially. Unfortunately, while this dynamic may contribute to relationship, tribal field and synchronicity, it can also be destructive. It is clear that human emotion is the engine that can create or destroy much of what is in existence. We need only to think of the lynchings that took place in the last century to evoke wonder that upstanding, church-going men could carry out such heinous crimes. Intuitively, we know that emotion played a principal role. More recently, one marvels at the collective hysteria that led to the imprisonment of many people, now believed to be completely innocent, in the child sexual abuse craze of the 1980's and 90's.[2] It is evident that to give up one's standpoint on what is most valued and ethical is to be vulnerable to being swept away by a collective hysteria. The results can be lynchings, false accusations, and wars. Evil prevails when one's individual ethics are lost in or overwhelmed by a flood of frenzied collective emotion. The irony is that exploring dreams in depth confronts us with both the unity and the contradictions of humanity at a level not usually noticed in life. We strive to build connections to others, but also work to be individuals. Paradoxically, one brings the other into being. The more I know what I stand for, what is right or wrong for me and

---

1 Jaffé, *An Archetypal Approach to Death Dreams and Ghosts*, p. 172
2 John Stoll, NBC News: Dateline, 22 October 2004

how I need to speak my truth, the more I am connected to my community.

Synchronicity, in itself, is not dangerous, but it is powerful medicine and its significance must be weighed carefully. Anyone can become inflated and grandiose in the face of multiple synchronistic events. As much as building connection and relationship is emphasized as the cornerstone of this book, and of dream groups in general, it is equally critical to maintain one's individual standpoint. It is only then that a "Divine We" space can be constellated. It may seem obvious, but is worth noting, that almost all of the important events of human history, whether for better or for worse, are the result of individuals acting together in groups to produce results that no individual alone could have manifested.

As Jaffé points out, Jung linked synchronicity with emotion, or psychological libido. When the psyche gets extremely active, reality begins to shift and the archetypal field is constellated. The emotions that constitute a tribal, synchronistic field in a dream circle have varied possibilities. Usually love, in all of its forms, is first to arrive,[1] then perhaps curiosity, admiration, respect, vulnerability, passion and so on. These are the emotions that can lead to more conscious, numinous and ultimately, synchronistic phenomena. Let's not assume that synchronicity is a divine blessing of our activities. It is not. Though he did not use the term "synchronicity," Osama Bin Laden has spoken of the related events that occurred around 9-11. He was especially pleased that peasant women who did not know anything about the impending attack on the United States nevertheless dreamed about it ahead of time. He considered this a sign, as he said, that, "Allah is with us." Days before the event, I, too, heard five dreams that I later realized could be read to as predictions of the Twin Towers attacks. In one dream, early the morning of September 11, 2001, a voice announced, "The world

---

1 For a Jungian discussion on the subject of love, see: Guggenbühl-Craig, *Marriage: Dead or Alive, p. 186*

has ended." It is important to remind ourselves that synchronicity has to be viewed as an impersonal phenomenon, and that it is morally neutral.

This is one of the salient reasons I have mentioned again and again the importance of creating a safe dream circle, a space that is respectful of individual perceptions, while also creative, open and curious. Unless these parameters are firmly established, the group psyche can be a powerful means to a destructive end. Synchronicity is prevalent in dream circles because an archetypal field is formed in the room. Synchronistic events occur often in analysis too, but when six or eight people begin to dream together, the emotion, heat and fire of the underworld is remarkable, and can result in uncanny events happening in the group.

In *Threads, Knots, Tapestries,* I offer a few examples that have amazed and delighted both dream circle members and me over the last twenty-three years. It seems the field that is created by a dream circle brings synchronicity into sharp focus, and that the archetypes of Psyche and Amor are brought to life.[1] Psyche and Amor, Soul and Love, were inseparable after they met for the first time, and this epitomizes the core of the dream circle, the numinous depths where magic is witnessed. Similar dreams, matching dreams, astonishingly congruent life events and instances of strikingly similar dress and psychological issues, all are events that defy the laws of mathematical probability. There are too many of them, they occur too often, and they are just too unbelievable to be mere happenstance. And I hear it from dream groups in every continent and country I have visited, that dream group somehow engenders a level and intensity of synchronicity that seems unbelievable, and certainly unexplained. The observation of ubiquitous synchronicity is not limited to my work; rather, it seems to be a common incident in dream circles throughout the world. Dream synchronicity can happen in a single dream circle session or over the course of

1 See: Hamilton, *Mythology*

many sessions. Synchronicity may happen around outer events or be contained only in the group.

Please bear in mind that synchronicity is not serendipity (a happy accident or good luck), nor irony (something that seems deliberately perverse), both of which are features of dreams and waking life. An example of dream irony is:

"I see an ancient flask roll out of a dark corner in a medieval room. I know it contains the answer to all my questions about life, but it is sealed shut. In order to open the flask, I have to break it, and I know that will destroy it. At the same time, I know I cannot break such a beautiful object."

Here one sees the bittersweet quality of a dream in which a crucial answer requires a painful sacrifice. This kind of enigma, quite different from a "meaningful coincidence," is sometimes confused for synchronicity. In waking life, a person might experience this: "I had a bad day. An incredibly bad day. First, a motorcyclist turning left ran a red light in front of me, and I hit him. He was rushed to the hospital, his leg was no doubt badly broken, and his wife and mother screamed at me. I called my insurance company to report the accident, only to discover my insurance had been cancelled because I forgot to send in my last payment. I was feeling pretty devastated, so when I got home, I called ..... He has been trying to date me for years, but I have always kept our relationship on a friendship level. But the way I felt, I decided what the hell, I'm going to invite him over for dinner and then make love to him. I took a bubble bath, and prepared a nice meal. Then, over dinner he told me he had met someone very special and was planning to marry her. He was delighted that we were having dinner together so he could tell me. I was so desperate I asked him to stay the night anyway, but he politely refused."

While this is ironic, it is not synchronistic. However, the meaning of these unhappy events would benefit from serious psychological reflection.

One lighthearted example of synchronicity occurred as our group was wrapping up after a particularly difficult morning. Lots of tears were shed that day, and the longing for nurturing and loving restoration of the soul was almost overpowering. One dreamer had explored a dream about an Asian man, perhaps a lama, who seemed to offer the promise of something nourishing, whether Buddhism, meditation, art, or something entirely unknown, she could not say. A profound silence followed this reflection, when suddenly the door to my office flew open. This was remarkable, in part because the intruder had to go through two closed doors to my inner group room, and also because I cannot think of another time in seventeen years that anyone ever opened the first and second doors without knocking. There in the open door stood an Asian man holding three or four large, white paper sacks of Thai food. Extending them to us, he called out, "Your lunch is here!" We exploded in laughter, and I am afraid the poor man left rather confused.

This synchronicity appeared over several years:

The dream group met every other week for three hours and was made up of clergy and therapists. At a certain point, the group accepted a new person who didn't fit that profile: a woman who had been an architect, but now worked in her husband's medical practice. She fit in fine, but after following her dreams for a year or two, she experienced what often happens in analysis or a dream group. She decided to live her life in a different way, one that was more in keeping with her talents and values. She was soon accepted by an art school in New York, and moved away. Before she left, she asked if we would save a seat for her, since she planned to return to our city.

Her replacement was a therapist who displayed an unusually keen interest in art; she designed and decorated rooms, wore artistic clothes, and even dreamed about artists. In fact, on her first day in group, she shared a dream about a young man to whom she was attracted, who was himself an artist. All this certainly indicated that she had an unseen artist aspect that sought expression, but the artist in her dream was an actual person, and another member of the group had also dreamt about him that day. He was the second dreamer's son, whom the new member had met at an art show the weekend before. So here we were with two dreams that featured the same young man.

Later that day, the mail arrived, and I received a letter from our art student in New York. In the letter, she told about discovering an amazing coincidence in our group: she found out that a granddaughter who was having some trouble in school had been helped enormously by an understanding young art teacher who proved to be our second dreamer's son. She went on to write that her own two sons had also realized that the three of them had attended high school together. She was floored by this network of connections, not knowing that we had heard two dreams about that same man that very day. And here we had a letter about him, too.

Eventually the artist came back to the Dallas/Ft. Worth area and to the dream circle. The day she returned, another member had this dream:

> *I am looking at the Madonna and have a strong spiritual feeling of awe. Eventually, I see that she has an opening, a space in the area of her womb. When I look into the empty space, there is a whole different dimension beyond.*

Before this dream could even be completely told, the artist got very wiggly in her chair – a definite sign that the spirit is moving. She said excitedly, "That is just like an art exhibit I helped install in New York. We hung Madonnas on the wall with open cavities where their wombs would be. As we installed the art, we made holes in the walls to line up with the openings in the sculptures so you could see into the next room where there were more Madonnas positioned throughout the space.

We mused about this "coincidence," knowing that the synchronicity had taken all of us to a magical, mysterious place, a place that reminds one of gods and goddesses, and is impossible to explain fully. Every time I told that story, once in Portland, Oregon, once in Zurich and once at Pacifica Graduate School, a member of the audience chimed in with a synchronicity that clearly connected with the story. The sculpture a woman had made the previous day of a Madonna with a cave for a womb, the psychologist who guided a woman into a visualization that resulted in meeting the Madonna in a grotto, and a woman who heard the New York artist who created the original exhibit interviewed on the radio on the way home from my talk, all these added to the breadth and depth of the dream narrative and the sense of mystery.

Then, in 2008, another dream in the series came to this same dream group:

> *I look at my vagina by holding a mirror between my legs, and realize that I can see all the way into myself, where there is another world, one that is numinous and holy.*

This image, even over ten years later, seemed to echo the earlier dream and the synchronistic events that surrounded it. In this instance, the dream seemed even more personal and intimate, almost embarrassing to share with others, as is often the case with deeply spiritual experiences. This group knew to hold the dream as sacred, and reflected on the aspect of the archetypal feminine goddess, whose sexuality is part of her mystery, her essence. And in early 2009, a new member of dream group, the first new member in about five years, had this dream:

> *A doctor examines me and stitches a minor wound on the sole my foot. I say, "Don't touch that place, it will hurt." "No, it won't," the doctor says. She pokes my sole with a spoon, and I see a deep hole – but it doesn't hurt. Then, when she scoops even more flesh out of the sole of my foot, I can see all the way inside myself, into a space that glows with soft luminescence.*

Again, whether the dream uses the image of the person or the divine feminine, we find the theme of seeing deeply inside oneself, where there is another dimension, one that is filled with mystery. That is the quintessential connecting element in these dreams. In this case, the pun of "sole" and "soul" was not lost on the dream circle. The image of "digging deeply into oneself" was also discussed as an appropriate metaphor for exploring one's internal world, seeking to discover the divine within.

These stories bend and flow into one another like a Möbius strip with no beginning and no end. To honor these startling experiences, I decided to hold my first dream retreat in Einsiedeln, Switzerland, where there is a famous shrine to the Black Madonna.[1]

There, synchronicity defied time, reason and our understanding of reality (so far). One never knows when or what will emerge to clarify or confuse the issue. But it seems obvious that synchronicity is more likely to occur when an archetypal tribal field is created and connection manifests through intimacy.

Exercise

Record and discuss some of the synchronicities your group has experienced. Gather your impressions about what those synchronicities signify for the dream group. (As long as this is plainly characterized as speculation, it is all right to conjecture about thoughts and musings.) Explore together what effect the synchronicity had on you. If you're willing, I would be grateful for any examples you might send me. Please direct them to my web site, which is listed in the back of this book. I appreciate all material you are willing to share with me.

---

1 For more on the Black Madonna archetype see: Gustafson (ed.), *The Moonlit Path: Reflections on the Dark Feminine* and Gustafson, *The Black Madonna of Einsiedeln*.

The Dream in Retrospect

One young Lakota woman, a leader of her community, shared this story:

> "My grandfather had this dream when he was a young man, before he married and had children:
>
> *'The third born of the third born will be called The Stars are Hers.'*
>
> My mother was my grandfather's third born, and I am my mother's third child. I was given the name The Stars are Hers, just as my grandfather's dream told him."

I don't know for sure if this story is literally true, but even if it is embellished, it reflects the mythological and cultural importance dreams have in Lakota life. Dreams repeated over a long span of time are thought especially worthy, and are given significant respect. Unfortunately, since our culture has not honored dreams for generations as the Lakota have, the same respect for a grandparent's dream in mainstream America would be unlikely.

Nevertheless, The Stars are Hers' dream story illustrates that dreams are unrelated to the ego's sense of time, that they comment objectively on outer events and other people's lives, and that it is important to take note of them over time.

This is another example that illustrates why it is so important to leave open areas of dream work that might seem untidy, or too pat and obvious. A dream may not fulfill its destiny or make itself understood for many years.

On occasion, dreams prepare us in advance for events about which we have no prior knowledge; dreams also portray past events, events that haven't happened, and events that may never happen. It is not possible to overestimate the complexity, diversity and intricacy of dreams. They can collapse shades of meaning into a single symbol, they can adroitly humor, push us, and comment on us – all at the same time. They simply live in mystery in the transitional world, where mist and fog cloud precise understanding.

I offer a final exercise for each group meeting: leave at least one question about a dream open on the table when you close. Let unanswered questions have a place of honor in the dream group setting. You who seek insight, work to balance yourselves by appreciating the value of the humble phrase, "I don't know."

The Tribal Dream

Your dream can have as great an impact on me as my own dream, or your dream's impact on you. Together, our dreams might begin to "talk" to one another by presenting similar or even duplicate images. Or one dream in the dream circle may serve as a theme for the whole group over a period of time. There might be a character in my dream who provides me with factual information, and instead of that character playing a part of me, I might be dreaming about another actual person's waking life. For example, it is not uncommon for a relative or close friend to dream about a person just as she dies; it is only later, after hearing news of that death, that the dreamer realizes what the dream was saying. This does not mean that all dreams of a person dying are in fact true. More often, when someone I know dies in the narrative of my dream, it suggests that an aspect of me symbolized by that the person is dying or needs to die. It is possible to dream someone is in danger and later discover that the dream held an apparent truth, but it's a good idea not to jump to conclusions. The point is, in each of these cases it's clear that our dreams are interwoven with those of other dreamers.

In native cultures, a dream could offer information for the entire tribe, and dreams in general were considered the property of the entire community. We of the post-modern world dream in precisely the same way. This layer of the psyche is what I have termed the Tribal Field.[1] It denotes an aspect of the unconscious that is nei-

---

1 Castleman, *Op. Cit.*, pp. 60-62

ther personal nor collective, but relational and communal: Tribal. Over the years, I have connected with others who have been able to understand and share this view. Sometimes I have heard nearly identical dreams in back-to-back sessions of analysands who share nothing in common other than being in analysis with me. So the Tribal Field, as I understand it, is not something that can be explained by a simple formula. It's normal to dream about those we are close to, but it can be surprising, even disturbing, to realize that we are interlaced with people we've never met, but lack similar connection to people we know rather well.

When I read Jung or Jungian writers, and observe society, whether in my own neighborhood or in foreign countries, I see the tribal field among us. In a recent dream class exercise in Zurich, I asked forty-five students to select a partner that they didn't know at all. We repeated the activity four or five times, my intention being, in addition to the goal of the exercise, to introduce students to each other so they could begin to establish relationships. On the last round I noticed something odd, so I asked some of the pairs to stand. The first duo was two tall, slim women, both of whom had long, grey hair and both of whom were wearing purple. The next pair was two men of almost the same height, both wearing cream-colored slacks and black and white plaid shirts. The next dyad was two women, one of whom wore a black top with red slacks, while the other wore a red top with black slacks. This similarity was demonstrated through the entire group, with one exception: a pair that had no detectable commonality of clothing, age, height, etc. As we marveled at how this could happen, the dyad that had no apparent sameness spoke up. "We know what our connection is: we both have French as our mother tongue; we did the exercise in French instead of English." Out of the forty-five students, only one other spoke French as a native language. It was a striking example of one of the myriad ways the tribal field is in evidence.

Now when I see a new person for analysis, or for dream group, I look for evidence of the tribal field in the first session. I notice that I no longer feel optimistic about our future work unless a rather uncommon connection is evident. Usually, I try not to take these analysands, preferring to send them to someone with whom they will likely have a better outcome. For example, I recently interviewed a fellow cancer survivor who had lived in the same small town where had I lived (in another state far from Texas), and who presented with a core psychological issue very close to my own. She works in a healing profession, is fascinated with a particular culture (as I am), is my age, and was referred by a close friend through an odd chain of circumstances. I did not relate these synchronicities to her, but took note privately that in this narrative, overlapping congruencies were evident. I understand that such stories are confusing, because the need to protect confidentiality and their convoluted nature make them almost impossible to communicate fully. In sharing dreams and personal histories, you will begin to see the interwoven matrix that sharing dreams together can evoke. It is useful to ask, from time to time, "What is our glue?"

On the first night of each dream retreat, I ask that someone share a recent dream that seems to have some tribal qualities. I explain that a tribal dream feels bigger than the dreamer. (One example is, "Dancing on the Graves," the dream recounted at the beginning of this handbook, which has a universal quality and addresses a human issue; it is pertinent to many, if not all who hear it.) Then we select by "chance" the tribal dream we will hear much the same way that one throws coins to cast the *I Ching*[1], knowing that destiny will select our material. Using the tribal dream as a theme, we will work with it throughout the retreat, because somehow, this theme, unknown before the gathering, will carry the circle along to a shared, sacred space where dreamer and witnesses begin a soul relationship.

---

1. Wilhelm & Baynes, *The I Ching or Book of Changes*

Your circle will have tribal dreams, and they will raise issues and themes about which we all want to talk. Everyone will be energized by hearing them, because they are dreams that demand an audience greater than just the dreamer. The "Madonna" and "holy inner dimension" dreams cited in the chapter on synchronicity are such examples, dreams that seem meant to be shared with more than the dreamer.

In rare cases, one person will have a dream for a person other than herself, and the two, the dreamer and the one for whom the dream was meant, will "know" together that this has happened. Because I am an analyst and have heard many dreams about myself over the years, it is not uncommon that some dream material I hear feels like a coded message to me of which the dreamer is unaware. I do not share this information except in very rare cases, but dream groups and retreats will spend a significant period of time processing such material, as it is valuable and fascinating to all.

There are numerous examples of synchronicity involving more than one person, which is one way the tribal field manifests. Many examples are cited throughout Jung's *Collected Works.* Now that the Philemon Foundation[1] is publishing more of Jung's seminars and letters, one can read about many additional types of cluster synchronicity within couples, families and other groupings. I think of the tribal field as an area bounded by love, where the underworld of inner connection shows its face. How many times have we heard in descriptions of spiritual experiences, "We are all one, we are all connected"?

Nature seems to form clusters as well: trees grow together as forests, planets constellate in solar systems, giraffes gather in herds and dandelions convene all over my back yard, and these are only a few examples of the way natural elements occur as multiples. Perhaps there is a form of attraction that science has not yet discovered. Theorizing about how something happens, like planets clustering

1 www.philemonfoundation.org

around a sun because of gravitational pull, does not answer the ultimate question: Why? Why is there gravity? Why planets? What organizing principal is behind this?

The tribal element emerges in the ways described here, but in other ways, too. If we do not know just why or how it emerges, that fact does not change. This territory is largely unexplored in the post-modern world, but perhaps your dream circle will find new ways to bring this lost and ancient part of human relationship to greater consciousness.

EXERCISE

Time to speculate: perhaps your group is ready for an "intuitive discussion". What is your sense about the connections between you? If they have been vivid and synchronistic, can you imagine how that happened, and why? Where does your dream group go from here? What deep connections have formed between you? What is the name of your tribe? How will you chose whether to continue or terminate your Sacred Dream Circle? I welcome your thoughts.

Appendix A

Should We Engage a Professional Psychologist?

Dream groups take many different shapes and forms. Some have leaders, some do not. Some are led by people adept in dream work, others are not. Whatever is true in your case, dream groups can be productive and insightful if some important rules are followed.

I recommend, if it is possible, that you engage a Jungian analyst or a Jungian-orientated therapist to assist in the development of your dream group. If you don't live near a professional who works within a Jungian framework, you could contact one to come for a weekend to help you start your group, and to visit occasionally.

Why the emphasis on finding a Jungian analyst or therapist? Jungians offer a well-differentiated palette for the understanding of dreams. Ordinarily, they study this art at length, and understand dreams from many angles, including mythological, cultural, collective and personal. Most analysts or therapists who work within a Jungian framework will already have heard a great many dreams; this helps them facilitate a dream circle even if they have never done so in the past. Typically, Jungians are skilled at helping dreamers understand their dream images in a way that is more thorough and diverse than other approaches. Even though dream studies are sometimes seen as pseudoscience, dreams, like any other natural phenomena, can be recorded, observed, studied and amplified.

One would not ignore or make fun of the weather because it defies normal understanding now and then. Over time, properly trained observation and respect will lead to greater insight and clarity about dreams (as well as about the weather).

Dreams are, actually, hard work. It is far too easy to overlook subtle but vital clues if one assumes that the meaning of a dream is obvious. It is too often human nature to grab for interpretations and misunderstand the significance of a dream when professional guidance is lacking. Even with a leader, Jungian analyst or not, interpretations are tricky and need to be teased out of frequently complex material with patience and real care. Interpretations tend to reduce the understanding of dreams; amplifications generally expand the understanding of dreams.

For groups without professional leaders: I strongly recommend you avoid the interpretation of dreams. Members of any dream group need a safe place to share, clarify and explore imagery, they do not need to hear what other members think the dream means. If you are compelled to pounce on dream material, then at least have the courtesy to pounce only on your own. Work to see your dream as material that is about you, your story and what you need to hear. If you have heard another's dream, keep in mind that nothing useful follows the ubiquitous opening statement, "If it were my dream it would mean … ." I have attempted to address this subject thoroughly in this guidebook; if questions arise, I suggest you consult a professional.

A Note to Jungian Analysts and Jungian-Orientated Therapists

Your greatest challenge will be to restrain members of your group from playing analyst. This can be especially problematic if synchronicities start to constellate, since this is a time when groups can lose their objectivity and fly along on a magic carpet of inflated certainty and dangerous contamination. Dream circles are clearly a group process, but at the same time, they contain elements of an individual analysis or therapy. In dream groups facilitated by a Jungian Analyst or Jungian-orientated therapist, something like a group analysis can begin to happen, and individuation processes might form around relationships. The safest and, in my experience, most productive model of working in the dream circle is for each member to work on dream material with the facilitator quite independently, much like an individual session of analysis. When the working dyad of leader and dreamer feels complete, then other members may be invited to respond to personal material the dream work provoked in them. This is *not* a time for them to postulate what they think the dream means. The more uncompromising you are about this, the better the group will function.

Also, if you haven't already, please familiarize yourself with the fundamentals of group process. It is essential to understand boundary issues in groups, to attend to the emotional flow of the group, and to protect or confront when either action is necessary. The family systems paradigm can also enlighten your view of group process, since participants commonly enact in group the same role they played growing up in their families. All group dynamics are part of the process as a whole, and should be monitored, discussed and sorted out by the group. One useful question to ask regularly is, "How is this group going for all of you?" Just as in analysis, any anger toward the analyst or other group members should be brought out in the open, rather than keeping it secret. (Recommendations for times when group members exhibit anger with each other are offered in several chapters of this guidebook.)

For your dream group to function in a way that creates the desired long-term intimacy, the study of group work and further training are strongly advised. Most dream groups last for many months, even many years, so beginning a group that meets for only six months may not achieve the results you seek. Questions about the life span of a group and other issues dealing with facilitating a group can be addressed to the American Group Psychology Association, which offers programs, training and publications to answer that need.

Appendix B

Sample Dream Circle Confidentiality Agreement

I, ..., agree that I will keep confidential all matters discussed in our dream circle. This includes, but is not limited to:

(1) The identities of all members of the Dream Circle group;

(2) Any and all topics covered during Dream Circle group meeting; and

(3) All details about the Dream Circle group process.

This confidentiality also extends to all matters the Dream Circle facilitator shares with the group.

If I encounter another group member outside our dream circle, I will not greet that person unless it has been decided in advance that we will acknowledge each other in public.

Acknowledging the critical nature in group process of privacy and trust, I understand that any confirmed breach of this Confidentiality Agreement will result in automatic and immediate expulsion of the culpable member from the Dream Circle. Any member who is expelled has the right to appeal to the Dream Circle group for re-admission. If such an appeal should be denied, I agree to abide by that group's decision.

Signature: . . . .
Date: . . . .

Bibliography

Aziz, R. (1990) *C. G. Jung's Psychology of Religion and Synchronicity*. State University of New York Press: Albany

Berne, E. (1996) *Games People Play: The Basic Handbook of Transactional Analysis*. Ballantine: New York

Bolen, J.S. (2005) *The Tao of Synchronicity*. HarperOne:New York

Briggs Myers, I. (1980) *Gifts Differing: Understanding Personality Type* Consulting Psychologists Press: Mountain View, California

Cacoyannis, M., Dir. (1964) "*Zorba the Greek*," Anthony Quinn, Alan Bates, Irene Papas, and Lila Kedrova. 20th Century Fox.

Cameron, J. (1992) *The Artist's Way: A Spiritual Path to Higher Creativity*. Penguin Putnam: New York

Campbell, J. (1987) *Historical Atlas of World Mythology: Vol. 2, The Way of the Seeded Earth*. Harper and Row: New York

Castleman, T. (1989) *Religious Traditions of the Lakota Sioux and How they relate to Analytical Psychology (Diplomate Thesis)*. C.G. Jung Institute: Küsnacht

– (2004) *Threads, Knots, Tapestries: How a Tribal Connection is Revealed through Dreams and Synchronicities*. Daimon Verlag: Einsiedeln

Chodorow, J. (1991) *Dance Therapy and Depth Psychology: The Moving Imagination*. Routledge: London and New York

Ciardi, J. (Transl.) (1954) *The Divine Comedy by Dante Aligheri*. Penguin Books, London

Coman, A. (1995) *Up from Scapegoating*. Chiron Publications: Wilmette, Illinois.

Cuddon, J.A. (1999) *The Penguin Dictionary of Literary Terms and Literary Theory, 4th edition*. Penguin Books:London.

Davies, S. (2002) *The Gospel of Thomas: Annotated and Explained*. SkyLight Paths: Woodstock

Erdoes, R. and Lame Deer, J.(F.) (1972) *Lame Deer, Seeker of Visions.* Washington Square Press: New York

Fitzpatrick, S. "*On the Passing of Battle Bell*" The Jung Page: Reflections on Psychology, Culture, and Life. 12 July 2006. www.cgjungpage.org

Grimm, J.L.C., Grimm, J.W., and Grimm, W. (Mannheim, R., transl.) (1983) *Grimms' Tales for Young and Old: The Complete Stories.* Anchor: Norwell, Massachusetts

Guggenbühl-Craig, A. (1977) *Marriage: Dead or Alive.* Spring Publications: Woodstock, Connecticut

Gustafson, F. (Ed.) (2003) *The Moonlit Path: Reflections on the Dark Feminine.* Nicholas-Hays: Berwick, Maine

– (2009) *The Black Madonna of Einsiedeln.* Daimon: Einsiedeln

Hannah, B. (1981) *Active Imagination: Encounters with the Soul as developed by C. G. Jung.* Sigo Press: Santa Monica, California

Hendrix, H. (2001) *Getting the Love You Want: A Guide for Couples.* Henry Holt & Co.: New York

Herman, J.L. (1997) *Trauma and Recovery: The Aftermath of Violence – From Domestic Abuse to Political Terror.* Basic Books: New York

Jaffé, A. (1999) *An Archetypal Approach to Death Dreams and Ghosts.* Daimon Verlag: Einsiedeln

Jung, C.G. (1969) *The Structure And Dynamics Of The Psyche: Collected Works, Vol. 8.* Princeton: Princeton University Press.

– (1971) *Psychological Types: Collected Works, Vol. 6.* Princeton: Princeton University Press.

– (1974) Hull, R.F.C. (Transl.) *Dreams.* Ark Paperbacks: London.

– (1984) (McGuire, Wm., ed.) *Seminar on Dream Analysis: Notes of the Seminar Given 1928- 1930.* Princeton: Princeton University Press

– (2008) *Children's Dreams: Notes from the Seminar Given in 1936-1940.* Princeton: Princeton University Press.

Kalsched, D. (1996) *The Inner World of Trauma: Archetypal Defenses of the Personal Spirit.* Brunner-Routledge: New York

Lopez-Pedraza, R. (2003) *Hermes and his Children.* Daimon Verlag: Einsiedeln

Meier, C.A. (1989) *Healing Dream and Ritual: Ancient Incubation and Modern Psychotherapy.* Daimon Verlag: Einsiedeln

Merkel, I. and Debus, A. G. (1988) "Newton's Commentary on the Emerald Tablet of Hermes Trismegistus" in *Hermeticism and the Renaissance.* Folger: Washington.

Myers, I.G. (1980) *Gifts Differing.* Consulting Psychologists Press: Washington, D.C.

Neihardt, J.G. (1932) *Black Elk Speaks*. Pocket Books: New York.

Neil, D. (1993) *Kachinas: Spirit Beings of the Hopi*. Princeton: Princeton University Press

Progoff, I. (1992) *At a Journal Workshop*. Tarcher: New York

Spiegelman, J. M. (2003) *The Divine Waba (Within, Among, Between and Around): A Jungian Exploration of Spiritual Paths (The Jung on the Hudson Book Series)* Nicolas-Hays: Berwick, Maine

von Franz, M.-L. (1972) *The Feminine in Fairy Tales*. Spring Publications: Dallas, 1972

– (1974) *Shadow and Evil in Fairy Tales*. Spring Publications, Zurich

– (1987) *On Dreams and Death*. Shambala: Boston and London

– (1991) *Dreams: A Study of the Dreams of Jung, Descartes, Socrates, and other Historical Figures*. Shambala: Boston and London

– (1996) *The Interpretation of Fairy Tales, Revised Edition*. Shambala: Boston and London

von Franz, M.-L. and Hillman, J. (1971) *Lectures on Jung's Typology: The Inferior Function, The Feeling Function*. Spring Publications: Dallas

Wilhelm, R. and Baynes, C. (1967) *The I Ching or Book of Changes, With foreword by Carl Jung*. Princeton: Princeton University Press

Wilmer, H. (1999) *How Dreams Help*. Daimon Verlag: Einsiedeln

Yalom, I.D. and Leszcz, M. (2005) *The Theory and Practice of Group Psychotherapy*. Basic Books: New York

Websites for Further References

American Group Psychotherapy Association (AGPA): www.agpa.org

The Archive for Research in Analytical Symbolism (ARAS): www.aras.org

The Encyclopedia of Mental Disorders, Copyright 2007-2008 Advameg, Inc.: www.minddisorders.com

The International Transactional Analysis Association: www.itaa-net.org

The Jung Center of Houston: www.junghouston.org

The Official Site of Marie Louise von Franz, sponsored by Foundation for Jungian Psychology: www.marie-louisevonfranz.com

The Philemon Foundation website: www.philemonfoundation.org

The Progoff Intensive Journal® Program for Self-Development: www.intensivejournal.org

Index

Tess Castleman

Threads, Knots, Tapestries

How a tribal connection is revealed through dreams and synchronicities

A companion volume to *Sacred Dream Circles.*

"Tess Castleman writes with enthusiasm and care about what Jung called the collective and personal unconscious, particularly its message delivered in dreams. Ms. Castleman gives a fine set of insights into group dream therapy as well as into the way symbolic language can help and inform an individual's life."

– Clarissa Pinkola Estés, Ph.D., Jungian Analyst and author of *Women Who Run with the Wolves*

269 pages, ISBN 978-3-85630-697-7

Ruth Ammann

The Enchantment of Gardens

A Psychological Approach

Ancient wisdom tells us that gardens have a healing, nourishing effect on the human soul and body. The garden belongs to the great archetype of life and is one of the few big archetypal images that are experienced primarily as positive. This positive experience is significant because the garden is a part of the natural and cultural human environment, and thus particularly influential in the interaction between human beings and their environment. This delightful book invites us to see and experience in new ways the abundance and variety of gardens and their influence on our inner life.

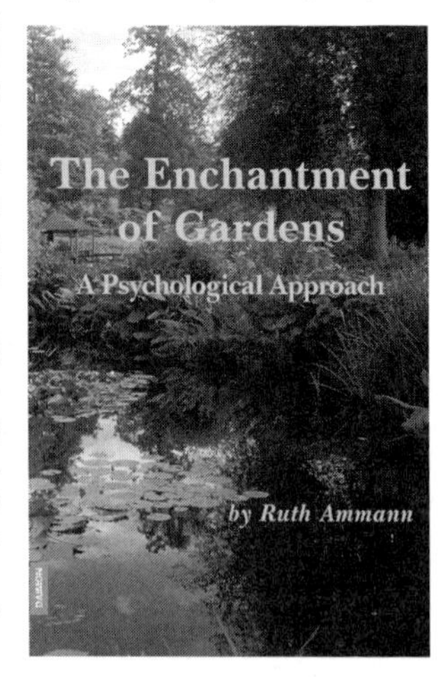

Ruth Ammann studied architecture and analytical psychology. She is a psychotherapist and sandplay therapist, and is a training analyst at the C.G. Jung Institute in Zurich. She is also an international lecturer. She lives in a house surrounded by a large magical garden.

168 pages, richly illustrated with numerous color photos, ISBN 978-3-85630-724-0

Eva Wertenschlag-Birkhäuser

Windows on Eternity

The Paintings of Peter Birkhäuser

Peter Birkhäuser's paintings frequently give form to overwhelming contents from the collective unconscious whose sense only becomes apparent when seen in the context of the spiritual predicament of our times. Birkhäuser was uniquely sensitive to the subliminal issues of the age. His whole career demonstrated that his special calling as an artist was to dedicate his abilities to a greater creative spirit and use his art to reveal, not only the crisis and infirmity of our times, but more importantly the reactions and healing impulses of the autonomous psyche. His pictures act as mirrors of the soul, where things hidden within us and our age become visible. In the major themes of the paintings we can observe something resembling a collective process of individuation. This is religious art, a manifestation of an image of God originating in the unconscious, striving to become real as part of a new consciousness. The artist's own personal individuation process becomes a gestation in paintings that circumscribe the birth of a new myth.

200 pages, hardbound, with 53 color plates, ISBN 978-3-85630-715-8

Regina Abt, Irmgard Bosch & Vivienne MacKrell

Dream Child

Creation and New Life in Dreams of Pregnant Women

Foreword by Marie-Louise von Franz

The broad scope of the dream material analyzed in this book allows the authors to touch upon many subjects associated with the nature of the psyche, not only those relevant to pregnant women. The careful interpretation of the amplificatory material drawn from a wide range of cultures also makes this an inspiring aid for the understanding of dreams, valuable to psychologists, doctors, midwives or general readers.

480 pages, richly illustrated, hardbound ISBN 978-3-85630-592-5

English Titles from Daimon

English Titles from Daimon

Laurens van der Post - *The Rock Rabbit and the Rainbow*
Jane Reid - *Jung, My Mother and I: The Analytic Diaries of Catharine Rush Cabot*
R.M. Rilke - *Duino Elegies*
Miguel Serrano - *C.G. Jung and Hermann Hesse*
Helene Shulman - *Living at the Edge of Chaos*
D. Slattery / L. Corbet (Eds.) - *Depth Psychology: Meditations on the Field*
D. Slattery / G. Slater (Eds.) - *Varieties of Mythic Experience*
David Tacey - *Edge of the Sacred: Jung, Psyche, Earth*
Susan Tiberghien - *Looking for Gold*
Ann Ulanov - *Spirit in Jung*
- *Spiritual Aspects of Clinical Work*
- *Picturing God*
- *Receiving Woman*
- *The Female Ancestors of Christ*
- *The Wisdom of the Psyche*
- *The Wizards' Gate, Picturing Consciousness*

Ann & Barry Ulanov - *Cinderella and her Sisters*
- *Healing Imagination: Psyche and Soul*

Erlo van Waveren - *Pilgrimage to the Rebirth*
Eva Wertenschlag-Birkhäuser - *Windows on Eternity: The Paintings of Peter Birkhäuser*
Harry Wilmer - *How Dreams Help*
- *Quest for Silence*

Luigi Zoja - *Drugs, Addiction and Initiation*
Luigi Zoja & Donald Williams - *Jungian Reflections on September 11*
Jungian Congress Papers - *Jerusalem 1983: Symbolic & Clinical Approaches*
- *Berlin 1986: Archetype of Shadow in a Split World*
- *Paris 1989: Dynamics in Relationship*
- *Chicago 1992: The Transcendent Function*
- *Zürich 1995: Open Questions*
- *Florence 1998: Destruction and Creation*
- *Cambridge 2001*
- *Barcelona 2004: Edges of Experience*
- *Cape Town 2007: Journeys, Encounters*

Available from your bookstore or from our distributors:

AtlasBooks
30 Amberwood Parkway
Ashland OH 44805, USA
Phone: 419-281-5100
Fax: 419-281-0200
E-mail: order@atlasbooks.com
www.AtlasBooksDistribution.com

Gazelle Book Services Ltd.
White Cross Mills, High Town
Lancaster LA1 4XS, UK
Tel: +44(0)152468765
Fax: +44(0)152463232
Email: Sales@gazellebooks.co.uk
www.gazellebooks.co.uk

Daimon Verlag - Hauptstrasse 85 - CH-8840 Einsiedeln - Switzerland
Phone: (41)(55) 412 2266 Fax: (41)(55) 412 2231
email: info@daimon.ch

Visit our website: **www.daimon.ch** *or write for our complete catalog*